"Dear Nancy: Thank you for sharing your wit, wisdom, and generous heart. You have left the world a more thankful place. I'm sure many will benefit from your gratitude."

—Bruce Feiler, author of *The Secrets of Happy Families* and *The Council of Dads*

"Sure, you could skip this book and go write a bunch of thank-you notes on your own. But you'd miss out on Nancy Davis Kho's brilliant, funny, heartwarming advice. What I love most about this joyful, life-affirming guide is that it feels like a letter itself, written to me by a smart, kind friend who truly cares about helping me be happier—and knows just how I can do it."

—Mary Laura Philpott, author of *I Miss You When I Blink*

"Gives readers the tools, the motivation, and the direction to write gratitude letters— and entertains them in the process."

—Christine Carter, PhD, sociologist and senior fellow at UC Berkeley's Greater Good Science Center, and author of *Raising Happiness*

the
thank-you
project

CULTIVATING HAPPINESS
ONE LETTER OF
GRATITUDE AT A TIME

Nancy Davis Kho

RUNNING PRESS
PHILADELPHIA

Running Press
Hachette Book Group
1290 Avenue of the Americas, New York, NY 10104
www.runningpress.com
@Running_Press

Printed in the United States of America

Published by Running Press, an imprint of Perseus Books, LLC,
a subsidiary of Hachette Book Group, Inc. The Running Press
name and logo is a trademark of the Hachette Book Group.

The Hachette Speakers Bureau provides a wide range of
authors for speaking events. To find out more, go to
www.hachettespeakersbureau.com or call (866) 376-6591.

The publisher is not responsible for websites
(or their content) that are not owned by the publisher.

Print book cover and interior design by Amanda Richmond

Library of Congress Control Number: 2019946185

ISBNs: 978-0-7624-6845-4 (paper over board),
978-0-7624-6846-1 (ebook)

LSC-C

10 9 8 7 6 5 4 3 2 1

FOR MOM AND DAD

CONTENTS

THE GIFT OF GRATITUDE

One summer day in 2016, I climbed the stairs to the guest room in my parents' house, where I had been staying for three weeks. I sat down at Dad's desk—the guest room, when unoccupied, was his home office and his Official Golf Channel Viewing Room. Directly in my line of sight was a thank-you letter I'd written to him earlier that year. My father loved the letter so much, he had immediately framed it and hung it over his desk so he could see it every day.

January 15, 2016

Dear Dad:
As you know, because you probably drove me home from the hospital, 2016 is the year I turn fifty. I have had such a fortunate life that I decided the best way to commemorate this Golden Jubilee year is to write thank-you notes to the people, places, and pastimes that have enriched my life along the way, and this week it's your turn. You and

Mom had to be the first two people to get these notes, for reasons large and small.

Thank you, Dad, for being such an involved, interested, and supportive father to me. Your years of work at Kodak to support our family are the tip of the iceberg. You were, in a word, present: there to pop flies in the driveway in a largely unsuccessful attempt to help your youngest kid get better at softball, there to comb and untangle my long hair after a bath while I sat transfixed by *Gilligan's Island*, there to drive to Syracuse and deal with a rental car when I got stranded en route between Rochester and Philadelphia during college.

I'm also grateful for the ways in which you were hands-off—letting me screw up and fix smaller predicaments often enough when I was living at home that I didn't feel over-whelmed when the big ones happened to me as a grown-up. Sally, Larry, and I all knew that our successes were ours to claim—you never made us feel like you were taking credit for them, which these days is a rare parenting trait indeed. I think your granddaughters are probably grateful I had you as my role model in that sense.

As a dad, you set the standard for men in my life. Which is why it never occurred to me to date losers who treated me badly (well, one guy in twelfth grade, but you didn't know about that, and it only lasted one "date") or anyone who tried to cut me down. You were always, always supportive of my ambitions, and your faith in my ability to achieve my goals, especially in my work life, was at least half the reason I ever did.

When I think about my fondest memories with you, I'd have to stack our road trips on top—back and forth from Rochester to Philly so many times in my college years, and the time we went to Disney World for your job when I was twenty. Even our last road trip, as we drove from Oakland to Mendocino in a blinding winter rainstorm, caravanning behind Andrew with Mom and the girls up Highway One—I thought we'd get blown into the ocean, but you just kept saying, "This is so beautiful! Wow! You're doing great!" until my nerves settled down. The time you showed up in Munich with almost no warning, when I had just moved to Germany for my first job out of college, and you gave me what I was too stubborn or proud to admit I needed: a big fat dose of home and validation (that I worked for a nutcase). Sitting in the pre-dawn hours with you in February 1998 as you timed my contractions when Maddy was on her way. And I don't know if you remember this, but I loved when I was little and we'd walk around the block together at dusk and sing "Me and My Shadow" and do our best fake tap-dance steps.

Even as we all get older, you continue to teach me things and set a standard I'd like to follow: downsizing and moving into your lovely townhome while you and Mom can really enjoy it; helping Aunt Noonie with her finances and household, daunting as that can be; continuing your volunteer work at camp and the fire department; and all the other millions of ways you help people around you without expecting anything back in return. Let me reassure you: we will ALWAYS need you and have handyman projects for you at our house, whenever you come.

Maddy and Lucy are so lucky to have you and Mom as grandparents, and I especially love how you and Maddy have your engineering studies in common. God knows Andrew and I don't know what she's talking about.

I love you so much, Dad. Thank you for being so good to me, always.

Love,

Nan

Then, I opened up my laptop and typed "EULOGY" into a new document.

Six weeks earlier, while playing golf in his Friday morning league, my eighty-one-year-old dad had fainted. He got up, finished the eighteen holes (of course), drove himself home (of course), and waved off my mom's concerns. Though my mom's worsening dementia made it impossible for her to adequately sound the alarm bell over Dad's fogginess and uncharacteristic confusion to any of their three kids, it was clear in retrospect that Mom knew something was off with her husband of fifty-eight years.

My older siblings, Sally and Larry, both of whom live near my parents, figured it out anyway in their regular phone calls to Mom and Dad that weekend, as did I across the country in Oakland. On Sunday morning, they called me to say they were driving to the house together to take Dad to the ER, thinking he had perhaps suffered a concussion. By Monday morning, we all knew what had instigated the fainting: an enormous, heretofore undetected brain tumor caused by Stage 4 metastasized melanoma, a merciless disease that had staked its claim via tumors in his lungs, kidney, and bones. There was no humane cure for a man his age at this stage of this disease. We could only make him comfortable for what would turn out to be the numbingly short remainder of his life.

Throughout the quickstep assault of Dad's deterioration from cancer, because I'd had the foresight to write my thoughts down and send them in a thank-you letter, there was one simple but fundamental worry lifted from my shoulders: I did not have to worry that my father would slip away without knowing how much I loved him. Not a moment needed to be spent in self-recrimination or doubt. I could put my energy into caring for him and helping him transition peacefully, surrounded by his family, in the home that he loved.

That letter created a moment of peace for me at a time when I badly needed it. And the solace I took from its existence reinforced something I had been figuring out since I started what I would come to call my Thank-You Project: it offered me, the writer of the thank-you notes, at least as much benefit as it did the recipients. I had been a freelance journalist for more than a decade by then, but this project was the smartest writing I had ever done.

Not the content of the letters, per se—I will leave that to the recipients to judge—but the mere act of writing them. Though I had sent the letters with no expectation of responses, I had heard back from many of the people to whom I had written, who were touched that, in this era of texting and emojis, I had taken the trouble to fill a full printed page with my thoughts about why they meant so much to me.

I never set about to make myself feel better by writing

these letters. But it happened in doses large and small, over and over, throughout that year. And thank goodness it did, because, starting with Dad's death, my Golden Jubilee year did not turn out to be quite the party I had expected.

Dad had been Mom's primary caregiver as her dementia worsened, and it was only after he passed away that my siblings and I grasped the full extent of her illness. It meant working together to figure out a way to honor her wish for independence and familiar surroundings without endangering her health and safety. As Sally said more than once, "We don't really have time to grieve Dad. We're too busy worrying about how Mom will make coffee in the morning." Throw in a heaping dollop of guilt that I returned to California after the funeral, while my brother and sister and their families who lived nearby immediately became Mom's hands-on helpers.

I had barely unpacked from my dad's funeral when it was time for my husband, Andrew, and me to help our oldest daughter pack up her square tonnage from Bed Bath & Beyond and head back east for her freshman year of college, three thousand miles away. While it certainly was not a loss to see our Maddy start her adult life, and our youngest daughter, Lucy, was still at home, it was a significant adjustment at a time when I was already feeling pummeled.

If you, like me, are in the middle phase of life—what I term "the years between being hip and breaking one" on my Midlife Mixtape blog and podcast—you know it's a time of feeling pressed flat by concerns over aging parents and growing kids and careers and health and maybe a heaping dose of "Well, how did I get here?" If you do feel that way, you're not alone. Labor economists David Blanchflower of Dartmouth University and Andrew Oswald of the University of Warwick have conducted research showing that a typical individual's happiness reaches its nadir during middle age for both males and females in the seventy-two countries they studied, before levels of psychological well-being start to climb again. It's the so-called Happiness U-Curve, which sounds like an awesome amusement-park ride but feels more like your stomach after four corn dogs, one Tilt-a-Whirl ride, and a bad session at the Fun House mirrors.

Did I mention that this entire Thank-You Project took place against the backdrop of the 2016 presidential election? Remember that one? Kind of stressful and anxiety-provoking. During the months I was writing my letters, I would scroll through the interwebs or flip on the television in hopes of mindless escape from my personal worries, and instead I'd see yet another example of what seemed to be a complete loss of polite civic discourse, proof that we were going straight to hell on skids.

And then I would fire up the Word doc in which each recipient had his or her own single-spaced page, take a deep breath, and think, "OK, how did my high school best friend save my bacon? Oooh! There was the time we went to the homecoming dance and I was despondent over my date and she dragged me to the bathroom and said, 'HE IS WEARING BLUE SHOES; THIS IS CLEARLY HIS PROBLEM NOT YOURS,' and then we laughed so hard our mascara ran." And the cacophony of my anxiety over the country's direction would quiet just enough to make it all bearable.

It turns out that the restorative power of deliberate gratitude, the delight that comes from knowing you will make someone's day when they read your words, the recognition that you—yes, *you*—are supported and loved as you make your way through the challenges of the world is a heady tonic.

To be clear: even if many of my letters got me thinking about long-ago events and situations, this exercise isn't about wistfulness and nostalgia. It's about taking a little time to dwell in the past as a useful means of taking stock of where we are now and reinforcing where we want to go in the future.

Months later, when I wrote "Love, Nan" on the fiftieth and final letter, I printed and bound a copy of all fifty letters into a book to keep on my nightstand. That was my last, best fiftieth birthday gift. When I feel low—because, let's face it, the news is full of things to make us fearful, I still fret about my mom every day, and for whatever reason the girls aren't thrilled when I try to live their lives for them—I grab that book and flip to a random letter or three to reread.

The reminder I get of all the different ways I have been supported throughout the years, the tactile heft of a book in my hands that reminds me that a whole team got me to where I am today, is powerful medicine. It leaves me, to use a favorite phrase cribbed from my friend Jill (Letter #10), "suffused with a sense of well-being."

But don't take my word for it. There's a growing body of science that has quantified the psychological and physiological benefits of gratitude and its direct correlation to levels of happiness.

Let's start with a definition of gratitude, courtesy of Dr. Robert A. Emmons, a professor of psychology at the University of California–Davis, and one of the world's leading experts on the subject. In his 2007 book, *Thanks! How Practicing Gratitude*

Can Make You Happier, Dr. Emmons defines two components of gratitude. "First, gratitude is the *acknowledgment* of goodness in one's life." It is the positive affirmation of the people, places, and things that make our lives worthwhile. The second component, he writes, is figuring out where that goodness comes from. "Gratitude is *recognizing* that the source(s) of this goodness lie at least partially outside the self." Understanding that many of the sources of happiness in your own life are outside of your direct dominion and acknowledging from whence that goodness springs are crucial ingredients in the gratitude recipe.

Research published in 2015 in *Frontiers in Psychology* found that an ongoing practice of gratitude basically rewires our brains to reward us for the positive perceptions we have of the people around us. That begets more gratitude and "elevation," a lovely scientific term defined in a 2000 article by social psychologist Jonathan Haidt as "a warm or glowing feeling in the chest [that] makes people want to become morally better themselves." Pour me some elevation, barkeep, and make it a double!

Dr. Christine Carter, sociologist and senior fellow at the Greater Good Science Center at University of California–Berkeley, which studies the psychology, sociology, and neuroscience of well-being, says, "All of our emotions serve different functions. We can say, in broad strokes, that negative emotions like fear and anger are more fight-or-flight-related and can trigger things like increased heart rate, accelerated breathing, and muscle tension. The positive emotions, on the other hand, reset the nervous system."

Dr. Carter points out that when it comes to stress in the modern world, our bodies don't do a great job of differentiating between lion attack and heavy rush-hour traffic; we experience both as threats, and our bodies and minds bear the prolonged strain. But even small expressions of gratitude can have a restorative effect.

"In today's world, where so many people feel stressed all the time, expressing gratitude is a highly functional way to get ourselves back to a neutral place," says Dr. Carter. "So if we express a deep sense of authentic gratitude, or even just a little bit of gratitude, we activate the part of our parasympathetic nervous system that can create a physical sensation of warmth in our chest or chest cavity." She says, "That starts the positive emotions working on our nervous system, helping us relax, helping us feel safe, helping us feel connected to other people."

Sociologists at the Center have identified myriad physical health benefits that accrue as a result of the regular practice of gratitude, from better sleep to more energy to improved asthma control. To put it more bluntly, Dr. Carter says, "if you could sell gratitude as a pill, you'd be very wealthy."

If it seems unfortunate that so many of us wait to engage in an active gratitude practice until we have experienced trauma, it seems criminal that people who are absolutely soaking in reasons to be grateful, as I was heading into the year I turned fifty, don't always remember to take stock and express thanks. We take for granted our freedom from harder realities we may have been spared, such as poverty, abuse, addiction, familial estrangement, and oppression, when, at the end of the day, so much of it is due to help from others and blinding good luck.

The good news is that writing a "gratitude letter" is one of the most common prescriptions from all those scientists and researchers for people looking for a way to elevate gratitude levels in their everyday lives. In fact, that's often how happiness scientists test their theories: they have the experimental group write a letter expressing appreciation to someone to goose their gratitude levels, while the control group is, I suppose, denied access to stationery. Just think: you can replicate the studies, only without that pesky MRI!

More than a year after I'd sent off my last thank-you letter, I was sitting on a patio at a party, explaining the whole project to Melisa, a friend on the verge of a milestone birthday herself. "How did you decide who to write to?" she asked. "Did you send every letter? How long did it take?"

I walked her through my whole project that evening. Months later, I was surprised to receive a hot-pink envelope in the mail with Melisa's return address in the corner. It turns out, I was one of the people to whom she'd written a thank-you letter.

"It has honestly been one of the best projects I've ever tackled," Melisa wrote. "The letter-writing project was many things: huge, exhausting, enlightening, stressful, soothing, time-consuming, emotional, and exhilarating, just to name a few. It made me insanely happy to put my love and appreciation on paper for my favorite humans. Receiving a text, email, or call in response to one of the letters was a bonus I never expected, but was blessed with, time and time again."

As I had explained to Melisa that night, despite its profound impact, the Thank-You Project comes down to three simple steps, done repeatedly: **see, say, savor. See** the people, places, and things that make your life richer. **Say** something to acknowledge your good fortune in your letters. And, by keeping copies of the letters to reread, **savor** the generosity and support that surrounds you.

With this book, I hope to help you **see, say,** and **savor** yourself into an elevated, more resilient frame of mind, using snippets from my own letters as examples to get you started. I hope to give you the framework to create a sense of well-being for yourself and to enrich the lives of the people you love, appreciate, and admire at the same time. I hope to remind you that receiving help and support with grace and humility is a gift you give back to your friends and family.

Consider it my Golden Jubilee party favor. Thank you for coming to the celebration.

CHAPTER 1

LINING UP YOUR LETTERS

Acknowledging the good that you already have in your life is the foundation for all abundance.

—ECKHART TOLLE

I am a planner and organizer, and I have never met a numbered to-do list I didn't immediately cuddle up to. But after five decades I have finally accepted that not everyone has a brain shaped like a yellow legal pad and a fresh ballpoint pen. This chapter will give you some tools and techniques to organize your letter project, steps that worked for me, and ideas for alternatives that may work better for you.

This Whole Chapter Comes with a Caveat

As with any long-term project, you can structure a road map for thank-you-letter writing like you have a PhD in organizational planning and still get felled by forces out of your control. In my case, I thought I would start my letters on January 1 and finish on December 31, just as the ball dropped in Times Square. How clever of me! How elegant! With my goal of writing fifty letters, my plan even built in two weeks to slack off, what with my being a Gen X slacker and all! Then Dad died and Maddy moved cross-country for her first year of college, and for three months I could barely sign a name to a check, let alone put in the level of thoughtfulness I wanted these letters to convey. There was a BIG pause in my process. I finally wrote the last letter almost seventeen months after starting.

If that happens, don't sweat it. Do you think anyone cared that their heartfelt, personal thank-you note arrived in May rather than February? They did not. Did anyone know about my arbitrary twelve-month timeline? They did not. No one is tracking your progress but you.

There's a catchphrase my husband and I have used since the early days of our marriage. Andrew is half Asian, which gives him a somewhat ambiguous ethnicity that has caused people to assume he is anything from Latino to Southern Italian to a member of the Tlingit people, depending on the dominant demographics of wherever they happened to meet him. He also likes to do absurd things to make me laugh. Either of those facts could have been the reason why, on that particular day years ago, Andrew gave his name as "José" to a deli-counter worker when he ordered his barbecue sandwich. When Andrew asked a follow-up question about takeout cups for sauce, the harried counter worker, trying to maintain order over the crowd of customers, spun on his heel and barked at him, "It's not always all about you, José."

It's not always all about you, José. José, no one even knows you're writing these letters. You thought you could bang this thing out in a month, and it took six instead? Good for you. Stop being so hard on yourself. You're doing a nice thing, and whenever it's done, it's done.

This means that my goal of fifty letters may not be yours. Ten letters when you have reached ten months sober? Twenty-five letters on your quarter-life-crisis birthday? Seventy-three letters because you love prime numbers? Make it so. This project really is one size fits all because you are the only one taking the measurements.

Make Your List, but Don't Bother Checking It Twice

Amazing secret revealed: the first step in the Thank-You Project is figuring out to whom you want to send your letters. WHAT? How did she know that? That justifies the cost of this book right there.

It's true. Much of this book is devoted to prompting you to think of the people who might appear on your list.

Here's a real secret, though: you don't have to write a single letter to start reaping the benefits of this Thank-You Project.

Simply looking at the list of names of your home team, your ride-or-dies, your hype squad is surprisingly reassuring.

Dr. Carter explains that when you acknowledge that someone else has done something kind for you, you are unconsciously accepting that they have incurred a "cost" for you. She says, "Research shows that thinking about it in those terms tends to dramatically increase our own sense of self-worth. It increases our sense of generosity, but it doesn't increase our sense of debt." In other words, we think, *If someone else has done something nice for me, I must be worth it.*

So, if you want to print out the list of people who have done nice things for you and carry it in your wallet to whip out and study while you wait in line at the DMV, or post it on your refrigerator, I certainly wouldn't discourage you.

To me, creating that preliminary list of people felt a little like planning a wedding or a party, in that I thought in circles. If I invite this person to the party, that other person should probably also be there because they are in the same general friendship orbit.

But unlike party planning, when you add someone's name to this list, you do not need to call the caterer or recalibrate your crowd-pleasin' chili recipe. Nor is it likely that leaving someone off the list will cause social awkwardness. Again, *José*, no one needs to know you are doing this. It's your project, and you are under no obligation to write a thank-you letter to that one guy with whom you are only friends because all your friends seem to be, but to whom you've never really felt a connection, what with his incessant talking about composting, or the Cleveland Cavaliers, or customer relationship management software. You're the boss here.

So, pick a time when you're well rested and well hydrated and have a good reading light—perhaps after you've read through all the chapters and have thought about who fits into the categories of family, friends, loves, mentors, and role models —and think of how you would answer these questions:

Who has helped me?
Who has shaped me?
Who has inspired me?

Here's another way to think about it: Would you be who you are right now if you had never met this other person?

Remember that shaping and inspiration come in many forms, both positive and negative. Then, start writing down names. Don't edit yourself yet. Don't worry about categories or ordering the list. Just write down the names that come to you.

And then stop. When I did this, I got to about twenty-five names, and then I thought, *Well, that's it; I'll never have fifty people on my list. I'm not sure I even know fifty people.* You might also worry about running out of names. Stick with me.

It Will Come to You

The act of writing these letters takes energy and thought—or it should if you're doing it right. And you are too busy and have too many demands on your time to pour that much energy into someone who, with the benefit of hindsight, you recognize was a nice person but was not one of your life-changing people.

On the other hand, the coffee-shop owner who greets you

with a smile every single morning, no matter how terrible your mood; who once jump-started your car so you could get to an interview on time; and who gave you a free coffee and a hug when she heard that your kid had been in the ER the night before? Maybe that's exactly the kind of underappreciated person you want to include on your list. Once you see how writing these letters makes those pockets of grace and generosity in your life more visible, the list will begin to fill up by itself.

Dr. Shannon Connery is a psychologist in Denver, Colorado, who decided to undertake a project to write 100 thank-you letters in 100 days. She was prompted to start writing in the aftermath of her mother's unexpected death. Shannon says, "At first I was just going to thank the people who had come to Mom's memorial. But after four or five letters, someone else I know did something really nice for me, so I wanted to add them to the list." Her list of names grew organically from there.

Shannon says that somewhere around letter 33, she panicked. "I thought, *I don't know sixty-seven more people!*" she laughs. "And then it got fun. I started thinking, *Well, who affected my life today, even if I don't know them?* I'm a runner, and I had broken my foot. I had to wear an orthopedic boot to get around. So I decided to write to the guy who made the boot!" Shannon says that figuring out a new person to write to each day forced her to look for the good around her, every single day.

Like Shannon, somewhere in the process of the year I wrote my letters, I expanded my definition of who should get them. We are shaped by so much more than the people we know. I realized I wanted to write down why I was grateful to the live concerts that sustain my music-loving soul, to the cities in which I had lived, and to authors whose books I reread every year. All of those things make me who I am, and even if some of those entities can never read the letters, it made sense to include them in my list. It brought me deep pleasure to think about how much I loved all those things as I expressed my gratitude for them.

It will come to you in the same way. Don't panic. Just brainstorm that first group of names and move on.

Set Your Rules

Lillian Hellman once wrote, "Things start as hopes and end up as habits." Sure, you can write these letters whenever you like, whatever length feels appropriate to the recipient, on a notecard this week and typed on a computer at the library next week. But if you write your letters at the same time or place every week, using the same basic format, you may find that after a few weeks it becomes harder to skip writing them. Because that is what we expressly do not want: an initial burst of energy followed by a miasma of guilt that you are now seventeen letters behind. That's not helping anyone.

In her book *The Sweet Spot: How to Find Your Groove at Home and Work*, Dr. Carter writes, "Habits are the way to best bridge what we know we *should* do and what we *actually* do." She adds, "When we make something habitual we free up the power-center of our brain to fully focus on the game strategy, a solution to a problem, getting our most important work done." Like the details you want to include in today's gratitude letter.

The more obstacles you put up for yourself—first you have

to find a new pen, then you have to find a box of cards, and do you even have any stamps left?—the harder it's going to be to create repetitive forward motion. Set some basic ground rules for the letters so you don't have to rethink them every time you sit down to write.

Finding a format, length, and schedule that makes sense for you gives you a better chance of integrating the letter writing into your routine until it becomes habitual. And, for once, wouldn't it be nice to form a new habit that you don't want to break?

FORMAT

I work at a computer all day long as a writer, and my handwriting at this point looks like that of a four-year-old wigged out on too much coffee. I could write a sonnet to rival Shakespeare, and my recipient would wonder why I had scrawled them what appears to be a recipe for alligator coffee cake. So, I typed my letters into a Word document. My friend Maria (Letter #9) has the most beautiful calligraphic handwriting in the world. If she were to type her letters, I'd feel cheated.

Make it easy on yourself. What do you prefer to do, writing-wise? Notebook paper and pen? Crayon on construction paper? Maybe you are more an artist than a writer, and it's not even a letter but a drawing of all the things you and your recipient have shared. Whatever speaks to you—make your thank-you-letter format that thing.

In the weeks leading up to her fiftieth birthday party, musician Kathy Valentine, bassist for The Go-Gos, wrote a thank-you letter to each guest she invited. She typed each letter, using a handwriting-style font. She then printed each letter on parchment paper and signed them. "I rolled up the letters and tied them with a ribbon and placed each one on the plate of the guest's place setting," Kathy says. (For her special guests' spouses and plus-ones, she wrote up a list of "50 Things I've Learned in 50 Years.")

Of course, her guests were head over heels (sorry, had to be done) reading their individualized, heartfelt letters at dinner that night. Kathy says, "It made my birthday spectacular."

LENGTH

File this one under "good enough is good enough." Maybe you have time in your day to write a six-page letter to the people you love. I hope you do. I did not. Between work and family and *Game of Thrones* post-episode analysis, I knew that attempting anything longer than one full typed page meant that the weekly thank-you letter would slip further and further down the to-do list in favor of anything that took less time and required less of my squirrel brain.

Real talk: I can focus well for the space of time it takes to fill one 8- by 11-inch page, single-spaced, but after that I need to check Facebook.

By the way, sticking to one page is not as easy as it sounds. Writing shorter is always harder than writing longer because it requires the writer to make tough choices about what to omit. Those of you who decide to go even shorter than a page have my deep respect.

Figure out what length of letter seems achievable and replicable for you. As the letters pile up, you will probably find yourself hitting a rhythm for what sentiments belong in the letter, and where, which also makes it easier to keep going.

SCHEDULE

I tried a couple of different approaches here—early weekend mornings, midweek lunchtime, just before bed—but for me, the sweet spot was late Friday afternoons, in that liminal time between the workweek ending and the weekend beginning. It gave me the whole week to think about what I wanted to say to this person and to sift through all the different anecdotes I could include to find the ones that best encapsulated what I valued about the relationship.

I would fire up my Word document and sit down to type. Someone once gave me a candle that is supposed to invoke the spirit of Jane Austen, and I would sometimes light that before I started typing. Maybe it helped; it probably didn't hurt. Thirty minutes or an hour later, I'd sit smiling at my Jane Austen–scented desk, rereading a letter that reminded me how lucky I was to know the person on the receiving end. It was a perfect way to slide into the weekend.

That worked, in some form or fashion, through fifty letters and almost a year and a half. Does that seem too fast or too slow? Melisa started with a good head of steam on her own thank-you-letter project, writing a few each week. She says, "I was all, 'OH YEAH! I'M JUST GOING TO GET THIS DONE QUICKLY!' and then I totally didn't. As I got into the harder, more introspective letters, they took more time and energy, and I found myself needing a break." When I checked in with her ten months after she had started, she still had a few names left to go on her list.

Shannon's one-letter-a-day-for-100-days pace was exactly right for her. "I felt like if I hadn't gone into this gratitude-on-steroids pace, I wouldn't have had such heightened awareness of its benefits," she says.

But if that seems like a heavy lift for you, fear not. Science suggests you may extend the happiness benefits of writing gratitude letters longer if you do *not* rush them. Research by positive psychologist Dr. Sonja Lyubomirsky has shown that people who perform acts of kindness tend to feel happier even weeks after they've performed those acts. Another study, by University of Michigan professor of psychology Dr. Christopher Peterson, found that writing a gratitude letter and delivering it by hand—always an option and something I did with a few of my recipients—can make you feel measurably happier for an entire month. Dr. Carter says, "There is really compelling research that shows it actually might be more powerful to just write letters once a month, and then really let yourself feel it."

Melisa pointed out to me that thinking about writing all those letters can be intimidating. "You look at the list, and that seems like a LOT of work," she says.

But you only write one letter at a time. And you're the CEO of this project. Pick the pace that works best for you and take the time you need. You could even stop for a while and come back to it, like I did. Relax: the letters aren't going anywhere without you.

So, What Do I Write?

We have finally arrived at the **see** part of **see, say, savor:** identifying the precise ways in which the people on our list have impacted us. I knew that for pretty much everyone whose name I'd written down I could bang out a whole letter that consisted only of sentences starting with "Remember that one time . . ." —and I've never even been to band camp. Those letters would have been appreciated too, I suppose, especially since by age fifty you don't take the answer to that question for granted. *Dear Amy: Remember that one time we organized a neighborhood talent show, only we spelled talent "Talant" on the big sign we hung, and our siblings stood in back and mocked us mercilessly through the entire production? No? I wish I could forget it, too! Love, Nan.*

But I aimed for something more meaningful. "Help" and "support" and "love" are such general terms. I wanted to think about what, specifically, each person had brought to my life.

When you made your list of people to write to, there were a few questions to mull:

Who *has helped me?*
Who *has shaped me?*
Who *has inspired me?*

Now's the time to consider, in detail, for each person:

How *has this person helped me?*
How *has this person shaped me?*
How *has this person inspired me?*

The answers to these questions are what you want to capture when you write. Good writers and good readers know that specific details elevate: "You're always so helpful and nice" isn't nearly as vivid or evocative as "Whenever I'm sick, you drop off chicken soup, and once I had a flat tire and you helped me change it, even though it was raining." (P.S. I love this person in your life, can you please introduce me?) In this case, it's not the devil that's in the details, but rather the specific contours of your relationship and this person's import in your life. Why not try to document them?

Kathy Valentine says that in the weeks before her birthday party, "I thought a lot about my history and past with each person I was inviting, and why I chose this person to come." She adds, "That reflection, and the fact that the fiftieth birthday definitely placed me on the other side of the life arc, made me want to express to each person what they'd meant to me: the things I remembered, the things I appreciated, the things I may have never said. I wanted each person who was there to know why and what I cherished about our times together and our relationship."

My blistering once-a-week letter pace meant that I had plenty of time to think about each person individually during the run-up to letter-writing day.

I'm a big walker. I used to be a runner, until I became a mom and realized that my precious exercise time was only thirty minutes long if I did my customary 3.5-mile distance at my usual gallop. (Let's be honest, I never galloped. It was more like the painful trot of a horse with inflamed ligaments.) But if I walked the same distance, I'd get a full hour away from the demands of my household and would barely even sweat. I have never voluntarily moved faster than a slow skip since.

My walking time each week was when I thought about those three questions for whichever person was on deck for a letter. I sifted through memories, let my mind wander, and generally tried to think deeply, with that week's letter recipient at the center of my thoughts. In some ways, the time I spent noodling over the person became its own prayer of thanksgiving, a meditation of gratitude.

Again, if you never pick up a pen to write an actual thank-you note, you are still reaping rewards during this part of the process. Researchers have found that an important by-product of gratitude may be an enhanced tendency to recall positive events from your life. In other words, you can train your mind to dwell more easily on positive things instead of negative things by . . . dwelling on positive things. This is referred to as a positive recall bias, or an ability to conjure up more pleasant memories than unpleasant ones.

"There is some theory and empirical evidence that suggests that gratitude makes you feel more connected to others and more satisfied with your relationships, which breeds more relationship-promoting behaviors that feed back into the positive loop," says happiness researcher Dr. Kristin Layous, assistant professor of psychology at California State University East Bay. "Oftentimes negative situations and emotions grab our attention first. It's evolutionarily adaptive for them to do that because if something is harming us, we need to address it." Dr. Layous continues, "It serves us well to re-train our minds— especially those of us prone to negativity—to look for positive events and to amplify their effect on our moods by actively appreciating them."

So, even when all you are doing is actively considering what you are going to write, you are rewiring your brain to see the good in your life. Can you understand now why I didn't want to rush through writing all my letters in four days?

You could think over those "how" questions for your next letter's recipient during your morning commute, when you're cooking, when you are on hold with a customer service rep from Mumbai named "Steve." You know those times in your day when your mind tends to wander anyway? Try to make it wander on over to your grade-school friend Julie or the brother-in-law who never forgets your birthday and see what you come up with.

You could also do it instead of counting sheep at night and get a better night's rest as a result. Research that Dr. Emmons conducted in 2003 to measure the impact of counting blessings versus burdens in test subjects found that those participants who were encouraged to think about the things, large and small, for which they were grateful reported a better quality of sleep each night than either the group told to focus on the hassles in their lives or the group told to think about neutral life events before they fell asleep. A similar study in 2016 found that an active gratitude practice correlated with better sleep and decreased blood pressure.

Maybe you want to write down notes for each person, or record your thoughts into your phone, or jot down a quick list of adjectives or stories. Or you might want to just think your thoughts and pay attention to the ones that stick around more than others. Once you feel like you have enough material ready, it's time to sit down and write.

LETTER OUTLINE

It is finally time to put pen to paper (or fingers to keyboard, etc.) and **say** what you have had a chance to consider for each letter recipient, to memorialize and express your thanks for this person's impact in your life.

How do you create rules around writing individualized thank-you notes to people who are nothing alike, and whose gifts to you may run the gamut from teaching you to drive a stick shift, to giving career advice, to calling you on your bullshit? It's a fair question, and one that may not have an answer. I just know that having a bit of structure helped me organize my thoughts before I wrote each letter, and having a sense of what I needed to include was easier than facing down an empty page and the edict, "Fill This."

The structure of my letters looked like this:

• *An introductory paragraph:* This was short and, for the most part, recycled for every letter, with a couple of minor tweaks to personalize it for each person. I told them why I was writing thank-you letters at this stage of life and how happy I was to be writing to them in particular that week.

True and weird story: When I brainstormed that list of names back at the start of the project, it was with zero forethought about when, on the calendar, I would be writing to each person. But at some point this whole project was struck by a spooky cosmic symmetry, and the week I would write to a given person would invariably turn out to be either their birthday week, or a week I'd see them in person for the first time in months or years, or some other major milestone related to the relationship. It happened so frequently that I gave up trying to understand it.

Including the intro paragraph about the letter being part of a larger project also assuaged my slight worry that recipients would feel uncomfortable to be on the receiving end of such a heartfelt note and wonder why I had singled them out. *It's not always all about you, José;* I'm writing these to a bunch of people, and I'm not planning to stand outside your door with a boombox playing a Peter Gabriel song tomorrow night or anything like that.

On the other hand, when Shannon did her 100-thank-you-letter blitz, she deliberately did not mention to any of her recipients that the letter in their hands was part of a larger project. For all they knew, they were the only ones to receive such a note. That certainly lessens any awkwardness that could stem from people's comparing notes about whether you consider them influential in your life. (An awkwardness I have now managed to supersize for myself by writing this book. Hiiiiiiiiiii.)

• *How we met:* It's nice to reflect on how and when someone came into your life for the first time and how the spark of the relationship began, especially for relationships you have had for a long time. Were you in the same cabin at summer camp? Did you meet in the HR office while applying for a job that neither of you got? Were you in the delivery room when this baby person was born, or do you remember the moment the adoption-agency employee placed that baby person into your arms? When I wrote to my friend Tiffany (Letter #23), I reminded her that for a few years before we introduced ourselves, we used to pass in the hallway of our daughters' elementary school, point at each other's shoes, and give a silent nod of mutual appreciation. Remember how you felt when you first connected? That's worth memorializing. Write it down.

• *Body paragraphs:* Here's where all my Jack Handy Deep Thoughts about this person got captured. I basically just filled the page with what I hoped were the most important aspects of my appreciation for the role they played in my life.

There was always a little bit of "Remember that one time . . . ," but my rule was that if I was including such anecdotes, I also had to include why that was formative or important to me. Back to those three questions: How exactly did that help me/shape me/inspire me? If I couldn't answer that, it didn't diminish the memory; it just meant it might not need to go in the letter.

Think about situations in which you have turned to this person for help, for advice, for companionship. Is there a common thread? What are the most memorable experiences you have shared, and have there been lasting impacts on your life from those? If you had a problem and were given one Phone-a-Friend opportunity, for what kind of question, encouragement, or dilemma would you call this person?

I generally had room for four to six paragraphs for this section. I found that a lack of material wasn't the problem; it was keeping it within my one-page limit. But hey, one page was my arbitrary rule. It doesn't have to be yours if you're finding it hard to stay within that container.

• *Closing:* I tried to close each letter with some future-looking thought about time I wanted to spend with them or activities I hoped we would do together soon. After all, the point of these letters is to capture a moment in time in a relationship, not to break up with the recipient.

That's it. It isn't complicated or super long, but once I hit a rhythm with writing the letters, knowing that I had to fill that structure for each recipient made it easier to organize my thoughts.

Here's an example of a letter I wrote to my friend Dawn, an eighties alternative music dancing aficionado, a gifted physical therapist who got me through a bad bout of age-related frozen shoulder, and an advanced camper, especially compared to my family, which, all our friends know, prefers staying in hotel rooms with high thread counts. This letter shows how that basic structure I used plays out.

June 29, 2016

Dear Dawn:
Back in January, with an eye toward my Golden Jubilee year, I decided the best way to commemorate this big milestone was to write one letter every week to thank someone who has enriched my life along the way. This week when I take you out for your birthday lunch, I'm gonna hand it over.

And I can't think of a better scenario in which to do it, because you are a friend who has set an example for me in making space and time for her friends, putting the effort in to make sure friendships continue to evolve. Whether it's inviting me by for a cup of coffee, getting the families together to play Telestrations, or suggesting a lunch on a Friday afternoon for us and the kids, you always impress me with the warmth and generosity of your friendship. Anyone lucky enough to know you would say the same.

I remember meeting you when Lucy and Abby were in kindergarten and you were carrying Baby Charlotte on the playground—maybe it's our shared New York State heritage, but I felt comfortable with you right from the start. It has been wonderful watching our girls grow up and find their paths. It's also been great to see the friendship between our husbands take root. I know that whenever we're over at your house for your splendid and generous cooking, everyone in both families will find something to laugh at.

I also appreciate that I am not the only person who feels that spending a night at the Cat Club in San Francisco is a good use of what time we have on the planet. Nothing better than a few hours people-watching and shaking our groove sticks to the sounds of the eighties, with whomever we've managed to drag along with us that night. If we ever get too old to be amused by Wendy in the beret, Randy with the brass-knuckle earrings, or random youngsters dressed only in duct-tape bikinis, all while DJ Damon spins Bronski Beat and New Order, then take us out back and put us out of our misery. My fiftieth birthday dance party was one of the best nights of 2016—thank you for all your help!

I say this in utter seriousness: your physical therapy for my frozen shoulder was one of the best things that happened to me in my forties. I was in a lot of pain, and then in one magic session I could suddenly move my arm again. You are so good at what you do—I credit you for helping me get back on track to a life where I can, in fact, raise my hands in the air like I just don't care. And you of all people know what that means to me—see paragraph above. The only bummer was that you were so good at your job that, eventually, our weekly therapy/gossip sessions had to end. Maybe I'll twist an ankle or something just for a reason to come back in. (UNIVERSE, I AM KIDDING—DON'T TRIP ME.)

We are very grateful to your clan for helping us through our camping adventures. The dirty secret of the "Khos Don't Camp" Kho Family is that we actually like to camp, we're just intimidated by the gear and the preparation. Ever since you took us under your protective wings, we've been much surer of ourselves and ready to see which beautiful spot you'll take us to next. It's a stressful time right now with my dad's diagnosis, but I look forward to the day that we can commit to doing another trip into the woods with all of you.

In short, dear Dawn, thanks for being a wonderful friend, a camping mentor, a dance hall queen, a gourmet cook, and a free-er of shoulders. You rock, in all sorts of ways.

Love,

Nan

Kathy says that when she wrote her letters, "each letter was very, very different and individualized. There were little moments that were lodged in my memory that the recipient might not have known. I wrote what I admired about them, what I'd learned from them, how it felt to be with them, what made me proud of them." Kathy adds, "I also wrote about any disagreements or conflicts we had and how we had managed to navigate those. I rewrote until I could make sure it fit on one page. I wanted them to be equal."

If at any point you worry that your writing isn't up to par, if you are unsure about what you should say, if you doubt whether anyone would even want to receive a thank-you letter from you, I'm going to ask you this: have you ever received a heartfelt, physical thank-you note from someone, sneered, "Well, THAT sucks!" and tossed it in the trash?

I'm going to guess no.

Similarly, you may feel hesitant to share your feelings with your recipients, worried you will overwhelm them with the rush and depth of your emotions. You envision someone opening your letter, skimming it, and thinking, *Is Jennifer dying? Why did she write this?* and then calling 911 for a welfare check. There's a world of difference between writing a performative thanks on someone's Facebook wall for the world to see and writing a more private, in-depth thank-you letter.

In writing these letters, you do make yourself vulnerable— by telling someone that you rely and depend on them, that they shaped you in some way. That can be a scary feeling. I would just say that in a time when the lure, tone, and omnipresence of online discourse make it easy to feel isolated from the people around us, even (especially?) when we're sitting in the same room and bent over our devices, it's a beautiful act of courage to expose your indebtedness in the service of deepening your connections to people who are important to you.

The flames of so much hostility and anger surround us these days, with people quick to presume ill intent. Maybe think of each letter you write as a bucket of water you contribute to the community fire brigade in order to cool and soothe the general atmosphere. If ever you were going to buck up and do something brave, kiddo, this is a good time.

Of course, I cannot speak for every person walking the planet. But I can tell you that not one recipient of the many letters I sent took it badly. Their acknowledgments came in different sizes, varieties, and tempos—people process things in unique ways—but no one cut me out of their lives for telling them how much I valued their role in mine. If anything, I felt like writing the letters added a layer of strength to the relationships they documented.

In his book *A Primer on Positive Psychology,* Dr. Peterson summarized the responses he had seen to gratitude letters thusly: "In our experience with dozens of gratitude letters . . . they 'work' 100% of the time in the sense that the recipient is moved, often to tears, and the sender is gratified as well."

The people who get your letters do not care if it is Pulitzer Prize literature. They do not care if there are cross-outs or misspellings. They do not care if you write the whole thing on a piece of scrap paper. What your recipients care about is that you took the time to acknowledge their big-heartedness, that you included the story of how you bonded when you played soccer together in middle school, that you have taken note of the volunteer work they perform through their mosque and how it has been an inspiration for you to get more involved in your own community.

What you write will be perfect. Because you took the time to write it.

MAKIN' COPIES

I can't emphasize the importance of this step enough, probably because I was so surprised to learn how much it did for me.

Make a physical copy of every letter you write, for yourself, because you will **savor** the bejeezus out of these letters.

Just as making that list of names early in the process may have given you a boost, I promise you that seeing the finished results of your Thank-You Project, the actual physical mass of however many letters you decided to write, is powerful medicine. And it's one without an expiration date or copay.

In my case it was easy to create my own copy because I had the one Word document and just added a new page every time I started a new letter. I'd print out the requisite page, sign it, and send it each week. At the end of the line, all I had to do was hit "Print" on my fifty-page document to see all the letters together.

If you're writing by hand, it means scanning or making a photocopy before you send each letter. Throw those copies in a folder, either digital or physical, and just keep writing. When you're done sending the last letter, you'll have the most wonderful collection of writing anyone could ever produce for you. And you'll have done it all yourself.

I imagine a person could have a lot of fun with the cover

and book design. I am disadvantaged in that regard. The last time I had any aspirations to pursue graphic design was in high school art class in 1982, when the grade I earned crystallized my decision to major in business. So, I took the easy route: when I was done with my letters, I had them printed and bound by a local copy shop, with a plain black-and-white cover. Yes, even choosing a colored font for the title page proved more aesthetically challenging than I could handle.

But you could go crazy on the design features of your book here—the cover, the binding, the layout. Given the love and detail of what will be contained inside, your letter collection would be worth learning the craft of book-binding over. Or you could have your book custom made by the print-on-demand services out there that convert your writing to printed books. It'll have a spine and everything.

You could also skip the design step altogether and just put all the letters into a box or a folder you buy at the drugstore. Hands up for the Trapper Keeper/Pee Chee crowd.

The point is to keep the letters together and keep them handy.

I keep my Thank-You Letter book on the bottom shelf of my nightstand, and I pull it out to flip through at random times—in the middle of getting dressed, before going to bed, when I'm procrastinating instead of folding laundry. Sometimes I just fan through the pages. Fifty pages of gratitude. FIFTY. Sure, I may have gotten jury duty or can no longer button the shorts that fit me last summer. But when I skim over the letters I wrote during that year, I remember I am doing A-OK.

The idea that thoughts of gratitude can drown out worse

thoughts is another emerging area of the science of positive psychology. Dr. Layous says she has collected five studies that tell the same story of gratitude's effectiveness at overriding negative thoughts. She says, "Gratitude is as good as distraction is at reducing negative affect," or the experience of negative feelings or emotion. "But gratitude has the added benefit of also boosting positive affect, whereas distraction reduces it." These changes in positive and negative affect also relate to other changes. Dr. Layous says, "Higher positive affect is related to a higher likelihood of participants stating they want to be out and be active or social in some way—both activities that could promote happiness in a positive feedback loop."

There's another reason I recommend making a copy, especially for people who are parents. I like to think that when I am no longer around, this book will serve as a reminder to my children of the ways in which I was connected and supported and loved in the world, an appreciation of who their mom was as a person outside the role of mother. They might not be ready to hear that as teenagers, but someday when they are older, I hope my letters of gratitude will be something to help them keep me close.

SEND THE LETTER. OR DON'T.

You've written a letter; now it's time to send your missive on its mission. Are you nervous about sending it? That wouldn't be unusual.

People who express gratitude to others tend to vastly underestimate the positive impact it has on the beneficiary. In a June

2018 article in *Psychological Science,* researchers Amit Kumar and Nicholas Epley found that those expressing gratitude via the act of writing gratitude letters (see, I told you it's the go-to tactic) significantly underestimated how surprised recipients would be about why expressers were grateful, overestimated how awkward recipients would feel, and underestimated how positive recipients would feel.

And that's a shame because that underestimation may hold people back from engaging in "prosocial" behavior, defined as that which is positive, helpful, and intended to promote social acceptance and friendship. Like expressing gratitude.

"Miscalculating the positive impact of social connections on oneself, or on others, could keep people from being prosocial enough for their own well-being," the authors wrote. Echoing a 1967 quote attributed to Lady Mary Wortley Montagu, "Civility costs nothing and it buys everything," the authors went on to write, "Expressing gratitude may not buy everything, but it may buy more than people seem to expect."

In his 2018 essay in the *New York Times* on the rise in suicide rates in the United States since 1999, behavioral scientist Clay Routledge wrote that "psychological literature suggests that close relationships with other people are our greatest existential resource." More than that, the science shows that it's feeling *valued* in a relationship that keeps us grounded, connected, and moving away from despair. How better to show someone the value they bring to your life than by writing it all down for them on one easy-to-carry-and-reread page?

Even so, no one says you must send these letters.

When you think of people who have shaped your life, there

are bound to be a few who did it by reverse example. The horrible boss who made you the management superstar you are now. The abusive cousin whose poor treatment of family reminded you to never take yours for granted. Sometimes just getting the lessons they taught you, and how that knowledge has benefited you, onto a page is plenty.

Or maybe there are people to whom you owe a debt of thanks, but with whom it would be awkward to be in touch, like former friends and ex-lovers.

Or you may just not feel comfortable sending it. *I don't want to draw that much attention to myself. Won't people feel obligated to write me back? What if they remember things differently? What if they receive it and think, "Who is this person?"*

Remember what we said, *José.* No one is paying attention to this but you. If you feel like writing someone a letter but not sending it, write it, then put the letter away. Job done.

Dr. Carter says, "The first purpose in writing your gratitude letter is as a reflective practice to put yourself in touch with your own gratitude, and to foster this positive emotion for yourself. So all the neurological benefits come from feeling the gratitude, not necessarily mailing the letter."

When Melisa chose the recipients of the letters for her Thank-You Project, she says, "In one case I wrote a lengthy missive to a former best friend who caused our relationship to implode in the nastiest of ways." The friend had done something so fundamentally against Melisa's values that it ended up reinforcing Melisa's ethics in the process. She chose to read the letter to a mutual friend who knew both parties and the whole backstory of the terminated friendship, and who validated her version of events.

Melisa adds, "Even though I didn't mail the letter, I finally got the closure I've been looking for, for fifteen years."

Melisa's experience illustrates a lesson that snuck up on me as well in this process: the ways in which gratitude and forgiveness are deeply intertwined. Forgiveness liberates us from dwelling over past hurts, so we can spend more time seeing the good around us and allow ourselves to feel grateful.

Particularly in situations where someone's mistreatment crossed a line into physical or emotional abuse, it may be hard to think in terms of gratitude at all. And even when you can, the road to true forgiveness can be long and rife with setbacks.

However, there are realms of emerging science that link forgiveness to improved physiological and emotional health and higher levels of happiness over the long haul. One study conducted at Virginia Commonwealth University quantified measurable decreases in blood pressure, heart rate, and stress hormones in people who showed an ability to forgive a romantic partner, while another from the same lab, summarized by Dr. Everett L. Worthington, Jr., Commonwealth Professor Emeritus at the school's Department of Psychology, found that "people who tended to forgive reported greater relationship quality and also greater commitment to relationships."

I do not want to minimize anyone's pain, but searching for the positives that may have come out of difficult past relationships and writing them down in a letter (sent or not) could end up being the first step on that road to forgiveness.

One of the letters I wrote was to a close childhood friend who had ghosted me after college. My Christmas cards went unacknowledged, a voicemail I left while passing through the city to which he moved was never returned, and while our mutual friends knew all about what he was up to, he had simply cut me out of his life in a way I found both puzzling and painful.

Even so, I wrote him a letter because I knew that the years we had been friends were foundational for me. During high school, he seemed to see the potential that I nearly blotted out through overeating, Aqua Net hairspray, and boy craziness. He used to ask me hard questions about what I truly wanted for myself, and those questions always stuck with me, even if I did not know the answers quite yet. So, I put his name on my list at Number 36. In the process of writing to him, I realized that my resentment about being abandoned was less important than my gratitude to him for believing in me at a time when I did not yet believe in myself. I wrote:

> We became friends in sixth-grade science class, and you were one of my very favorite people all the way through high school graduation day. You were a boy, yes, but you were nice, and normal, and funny, and smart, and you treated me like an equal. More than that, you seemed to see something more in me than I could see in myself. I wasn't old enough yet to appreciate it, but I recognized that you did, and for a confidence-deficient 15-, 16-, and 17-year-old girl, that was plenty.

I felt better for capturing those thoughts, and I filed the letter away.

The weird thing was that within a month of my writing

(but not sending) the letter, my old friend reached out via social media, and since then our friendship has slid back into its well-worn, if dusty, ruts. I am not sure I would have been ready for his overture had I not already written my way into forgiveness. Moreover, I found that after writing the letter, I was no longer all that curious about why we lost touch; he must have had his reasons. Did I write our friendship back into being? Maybe. My Aunt Noonie (Letter #7), who loves all things spiritual and metaphysical, would no doubt say there's a link.

PLAYLIST

Yes, playlist. Look, I have both a blog and a podcast with the word "mixtape" in their titles. I am that friend who insists on DJ'ing in the car when we drive, who has a Funeral Playlist already queued up on her iPhone just in case, and who often comes up with conversational responses that are song lyrics and must silently be translated into regular English before responding. "What's the time?" you ask. "Time to get ill!" I think, before passing it through the Beastie Boys filter in my head and answering, "11:15."

So, it's not so much that I wanted to create a playlist for you to write by for each group of names on your list, but that I couldn't prevent myself from doing it as I wrote this book. Some songs are inspired by my letter recipients in that category, some by the category itself. You'll find it at the end of each chapter, and you are welcome to play it for inspiration as you write. I myself cannot listen to any music while writing because the slightest boom clap makes me jump up and dance, or sing into the nearest hairbrush, which is hell on productivity. If you're like me, it's best to use the playlists like your baseball walk-up music, or save them for celebratory dancing when your letter is done.

A Word on Receiving

There's a necessary and fundamental mindset you must achieve to express your gratitude to someone else. You have to admit that you are a person who needs help.

That's not always easy. We live in a society that rewards strength, not vulnerability; bravery, not fear; self-sufficiency, not need. Our national holiday in America is called "Independence Day." Pee-wee Herman was a loner. A rebel. And we loved him for it.

But maybe what we need to heal the divisive and fractious times in which we live is an "Interdependence Day" to celebrate all the ways in which we are utterly reliant on one another. It could have its own host of parties, fireworks, and flash mobs set to "We're All in This Together" from *High School Musical*.

Fully appreciating the help and support of the people around us means poking our fingers into all the messy ways we have come up short in our lives. It means ripping off the mask of "I did it my way" to acknowledge that we have been someone who didn't know which job offer to take, who fell in love with the wrong person, who made obvious parenting mistakes until a wiser, more experienced parent gave us good advice.

This appears to be a particularly difficult challenge for men. A 2012 study on gratitude conducted by the John Templeton

Foundation found that women are more likely than men to express gratitude on a regular basis, feel that they have much in life for which to be thankful, and tend to express gratitude to a wider variety of people than men do. American men may struggle with it more than most guys. A 1988 study that compared how Germans experience various emotions compared to their American counterparts found that American men tended to consider gratitude an undesirable and difficult-to-express emotion; some even found it humiliating to express thanks. More than a third of American men aged thirty-five to fifty said they would prefer to conceal gratitude than to openly express it.

Which is the definition of missed opportunity, because study after study shows that people of both genders who express gratitude feel happier. In fact, a 1998 Gallup survey found that over 90 percent of teen and adult respondents indicated that expressing gratitude helped them to feel "extremely happy" or "somewhat happy." Dr. Emmons's research on counting blessings versus burdens concludes, "Seen in the light of this model, gratitude is effective in increasing well-being as it builds psychological, social, and spiritual resources."

So, there are two mindsets you might choose as you move through the memories that writing these letters will inevitably surface. One is self-critical. *What the hell is wrong with you that you needed advice all those times? Why couldn't you have figured it out yourself? How did you even get yourself into that fix in the first place?*

Taking that job in Germany that I mentioned in my letter to my dad, at age twenty-two and so far from home, so outmatched by a big job and crazy boss and the Bavarian dialect, made me the loneliest I have ever felt in my whole life. One day, I went out for a long walk to clear my head and promptly got lost. I had no money for a cab, no map, and no Pflasters to tape over the giant blisters that formed. I finally sat down in the middle of a sidewalk across from the BMW headquarters in my eighties business suit, with its giant shoulder pads and floppy bow tie, and bawled in public for a solid twenty minutes, alarming both passersby and their tiny sausage dogs. From a lot of angles, it was stupid of me to take a job where I could barely understand what my customers and coworkers were saying to me, and where it took a long-distance phone call costing 25 *Deutschmarks* I didn't have to reach people who knew me.

The other mindset is self-compassion. *Look at you, recognizing when you needed help. Look at you, figuring out that the specific person to whom you're writing this letter was the very individual who could give you the gift of good advice or a free ride or a hot pan of mac and cheese at the moment you needed it most. You were vulnerable, scared, and needy—and you knew who to call in for backup. More than that, you were smart enough and humble enough to receive.* When my dad showed up in Munich to check on me, I didn't pretend I was fine. I shut up and listened to what he had to say.

Letting others do something for you is not a sign of weakness. It's a gift you give back to them. If you have ever done something kind for the people in your life, you know this. If someone in your life has needed help you could provide but refused to take it, assuring you they could do it all on their own, you know it even more.

Leave the self-criticism in the dumpster and focus on the

self-compassion. You're flawed, but you know how to take help when you need it. That sounds pretty perfect to me.

By now you should have a good idea of how you might want to see, say, and savor your gratitude in a way that works for you. For the rest of the book, I am going to help you brainstorm the lucky people who will be the beneficiaries.

LINING UP
YOUR LETTERS

 A

For Beginners—M. Ward
Unwritten—Natasha Bedingfield
Don't Stop Now—Crowded House
Don't Panic—Coldplay
Do You Realize??—Flaming Lips
Line 'Em Up—James Taylor
I'd Write a Letter—Al Green
The Letter—The Box Tops
Please Read the Letter—Robert
   Plant and Allison Krause

 B

Ain't Wastin' Time No More—
   The Allman Brothers Band
Box Full of Letters—Wilco
It's Quiet Uptown—The Hamilton
   Mixtape/Kelly Clarkson
Ease Back—Amos Lee
The Call—Regina Spektor
Signed, Sealed, Delivered I'm
   Yours—Stevie Wonder

CHAPTER 2

FAMILY FIRST

We must take care of our families
wherever we find them.
—ELIZABETH GILBERT

When you sit down to write your first thank-you notes, there are a couple of good reasons to start with those who share your surname and/or your great-grandparents. You may live with some or all of these people and can both save big dollars on your stamp budget and contribute to your daily step count by walking the letter down the hall to drop it off when it's done. Another reason? They've known you the longest, and if you ever need a kidney or a loaner car, it doesn't hurt to have some goodwill in the bank.

The real reason to start with family, of course, is the outsize way our kin relations shape us. They brought you home from the hospital when you were born, or you did so for them; they stood shoulder to shoulder with you at your grandma's funeral, grieving in shared loss; they mercilessly insist on calling you by your childhood nickname of "Nubbin" even though you're forty-six now, something you find simultaneously annoying and reassuring. The people we'll talk about in this chapter are nothing if not overflowing in source material for your letters, so they are a great way to prime the pump.

I write this chapter understanding that the close and generally positive relationships I have with most members of my family aren't necessarily the norm for everyone. I know so many kind and loving people who have difficult relations with at least one family member: a sibling who has stolen money from their parents, a parent whose overbearing judgment has darkened their children's and grandchildren's paths, an uncle whose irresponsible behavior has torn the fabric of their family's existence. If you are completely estranged from a relative, you may think there is nothing to thank that person for—and you may be right.

And, of course, appending "step-" and "half-" and "former-" to the list of people that follows in this chapter can add layers of nuance and complication. Many of us have families so blended we could be our own menu item at Jamba Juice.

I still ask you to consider thinking about the positive aspects of what these relationships, in all their beautiful and vexing complexity, have brought to your life: an early need for self-sufficiency that means you can navigate hard times with equanimity, your determination to show your own children the love you didn't receive, or the incentive to create a chosen family from which you draw love and support now. If writing the letters, or merely thinking about doing so, helps you reclaim and refocus on the positive facets of your relationships with those relatives, you're nothing but badass in my book. Hats off for the alchemy you performed to turn that trash into gold.

Parents

The first letter I wrote when I started my project was to my mom. I figured I owed her that, having lived rent-free in her uterus for nine months. I have always been close to Mom, grafted to her hip in the waning years of the 1960s as she took my older siblings to Little League practice and Scouts and after-school bowling at Clover Lanes. Mom and I even look alike. When I gave birth to Maddy, Grandma-to-be was in the delivery room, and the first thing the obstetrician said after she caught my newborn daughter was, "Wow, she looks just like you. And you look just like your mom!" Anyone passing down genes with that much mojo deserved the top spot on my thank-you-letter list.

But the other reason I prioritized my mom is that she had been diagnosed with dementia about five years earlier, and her cognition was slipping away month by month. I hoped that by writing her almost as soon as I came up with the idea for this project, I would manage, for a short moment, to put a pin in the disease that was slowly robbing Mom of her words and memories.

You could, of course, start your letter to your mom by thanking her for the gift of birth, but I felt like that was so fundamentally huge and obvious as to be almost meaningless. Instead, my letter to Mom tried to capture some of the highlights of a childhood that was remarkable by being, by all standards, unremarkable. Thanks to the magic of reading memoirs, I have learned as an adult that all those things I took for granted as a kid were miraculous gifts. I mean, if you need reasons to appreciate your boring family, go read *Angela's Ashes* by Frank McCourt or *I Know Why the Caged Bird Sings* by Maya Angelou or *Educated* by Tara Westover. The predictable, loving, and comfortable home in which I grew up may have scuttled my hopes of writing a best-selling memoir about my tortured childhood, but I wanted Mom to know that, as a mother myself, I understood the hard work that had gone into creating our stable home life.

In fact, it was the solid reassurance of my mom's permanence that allowed me to pursue my goal to get the hell out of Rochester as fast as I could. From the age of fourteen, I was determined to be an urban cosmopolitan with a stamp-filled passport and a boyfriend who had an accent and maybe wore eyeliner—blame Adam Ant in the "Stand and Deliver" video. I could afford to be cavalier about leaving my hometown behind because I knew in my core that my mom would always be there to go home to. I could afford to take risks because I had a safety net built of steel-cable-strength love.

Mom's reaction to the news that I had gotten that job in Munich at age twenty-two was, in fact, one of the anecdotes I included in the letter. At the point I wrote her letter—almost thirty years after I had taken the job, and with daughters nearing the age I was when I took it—I had finally achieved the perspective to properly acknowledge what it must have felt like to Mom when I called that day.

There is one memory that will never, ever cease to astound me about you: when I called to tell you I got a job in Germany after college. You said, "That's great! I'm going to call you back." And you hung up on me, something you'd never done before or since. Even at twenty-two I realized what you were doing: gathering yourself so you could really rejoice at my news. A few minutes later, you called me back and did just that. Here I am at fifty, already a little freaked out about Maddy moving to the East Coast for college, and I. Do. Not. Know. How. You. Handled. That. So. Gracefully.

The generosity with which my mother let me go made all the difference in my life. The German job lasted for two years. I even got the boyfriend with the accent, though he never wore eyeliner. Then, I came back to the States to pursue a graduate degree in international management at a school where I met Andrew. If Mom had balked or cried or tried to talk me out of moving so far away when I called her that spring day in 1988, I don't know where I would be. But I cannot imagine it could be better than where I have landed.

There are other territories to mine for this one. Did your mother or stepmother welcome your partner into the family? Has she been an involved grandparent? Did she stake you when you opened a new business? Teach you how to make the perfect pie crust, for which you are now renowned? Or did she, in her choices, give you a template to avoid when you reached the same decision points? Does a strained relationship with Mom induce you to properly value the loved ones who are kind to you? That's all source material for this letter.

After I sent my letter to Mom, I called her to make sure she had received it. I was eager for her detailed reaction, of course, maybe a memory she would share about the kid whom she used to call Little Peanut.

"I did!" she said. And then, after a few stuttering attempts to converse, she went back to the topic on which her mind and mouth could still reliably coordinate: John Denver, and, specifically, a certain John Denver impersonator who plays a few shows in Rochester every summer. "You know he's coming back," she said.

"John Denver's coming back? He's still dead, Mom," I teased her. Mercifully, Mom's sense of humor remains, despite the disease.

"No, Nancy! The other one. He's so good."

I am sure that the love my mom had for me throughout my life is intact inside her, regardless of how clearly she can express it now. But did she understand when I wrote to her, "I'm saying now what I was too young and dumb to understand as a kid: you are the root source of the happiness and stability of my life"?

That, I don't know. But I'm glad I didn't wait even a day longer to write it.

I wrote Dad's letter after I wrote Mom's, sticking to my once-a-week pace, but I made a strategic decision to hold hers back and mail them both in the same envelope so they would receive them at the same time. They may have been married fifty-eight years by then, but why throw a ticking time bomb of favoritism into things?

My dad's letter reads very differently from my mom's, and although it was only the second letter I wrote, I was already starting to see that it was a useful exercise in identifying the precise ways in which I had received support over my life. Dad was not the guy you went to for a talk about your romantic problems or ideas of how to get the babies to sleep better or to discuss whether Prince Charles or Prince William was better suited to take the throne next. Mom had all that covered.

Dad was the guy who could talk through the pros and cons of a job offer, or suggestions on how to improve drainage, or recommendations for a tax preparer. More than that, he loved crisis. He thrived in crisis. I wouldn't say he welcomed crisis for his children, per se, but maybe he knew that when shit got real, that's when his fatherly superpowers were most clearly evident.

For that formative move to Germany, I was booked to fly from Rochester to New York City to Munich. My dad insisted on flying the Rochester–New York City leg of the journey with me. He told me he would see me onto the plane for my transatlantic flight and then turn around and fly straight back home.

I was mortified. One, I was twenty-two years old, and I knew everything. Two, what was he going to do, anyway? I found out the answer when I claimed my two cloth duffel bags at JFK, intending to carry them over to the Lufthansa counter to check in for the international flight. One of them had caught on a piece of metal somewhere on the one-hour flight between Rochester and New York City and had a tear the entire length of the bag, so the earthly belongings intended to see me through the next few years were spilling out all over the baggage carousel.

That's when my dad pulled a roll of duct tape out of God knows where, taped up my duffel, lugged it across the terminal, and checked it in for Munich. That. That's what Dad was going to do for me.

I have a theory that most parents have a personal super-power. My late father-in-law, Boen Tong Kho, was born in Indonesia, moved to the Netherlands just before World War II started, joined the Dutch resistance, was captured and held with other Asian classmates in a German concentration camp in Amersfoort, was rescued, and went on to earn two PhDs in science, one in the Netherlands and one in the United States, before marrying my mother-in-law in Pennsylvania and starting a family. His potential superpower list was a mile long, but the thing that illuminated him from within was his encyclo-pedic knowledge of every single college and university in the United States.

You could say to BT something like, "I went to Grinnell Col-lege in Iowa," and not only would he be interested in hearing what your experience was there, but he'd first inform you that Grinnell had an 18 percent acceptance rate, had been founded by Congregationalists, and that its mascot is the Pioneers. This skill was impressive enough, but it's the durability of it that I love. BT died in 2008, but there is still a Kho who can tell you everything you'd ever want to know about any college in the United States; I am married to that Kho. It's an endearing trait that passed from father to son and then, it appears, father to daughter. Our youngest child, Lucy, isn't old enough yet to have absorbed the entire corpus of campus knowledge, but she is well on her way. We often sit at dinner with a *Fiske Guide to Col-leges* on the table in case there is some question about whether a certain university was founded in 1803 or 1806.

Think about the situations in your life in which your father or stepfather came alive, like this was the role he was born to play. How did it benefit you—and how is it perhaps present in your personality or even that of your kids? That would be a perfect observation to include in your letter. Did your dad coach your Little League team? Teach you to play chess? Sit patiently through six hundred matches in the blazing sun shouting his support before your child gave up tennis without a backward glance?

I think it's also OK to acknowledge the places where a relationship with someone hit a rough patch—if you do it in a way that strives for perspective rather than revenge or vindication. These letters aren't burn books; if you do them the right way, they can be a chance to reframe and understand.

My father was a big believer in taking personal responsibility. "That sounds like a 'you' problem," was one of the most annoying, irksome things he used to say to us, putting the onus back on his three kids to deal with whatever he felt was within our abilities to resolve.

There was one "you" problem in particular that I knew I wanted to include in the letter. Andrew and I had combined our finances even before we got married, not because we were so besotted and in sync with one another, but because neither one of us possessed the minimum cash balance to open separate accounts at Bank of America. Between us, we had three or four college and grad school loans that we paid off religiously each month, tearing off the little coupon from the booklets we kept stacked on a desk and sending it in with our checks. When we had been married five years, we had saved just about enough to put down a tiny deposit on a tiny row house with a jumbo loan in Washington, D.C., where we had moved after grad school. What we lacked, and only temporarily, was enough money for closing costs.

Before Andrew even had time to voice an opinion, I called my parents to ask if we could borrow it from them. They weren't wealthy, but I believed they could spare the relatively small amount we needed. Besides, I would be paying them back in a month or two, tops.

I placed the call, and my father said no. "No." He said no.

The only elaboration Dad gave was, "I think you and Andrew will feel better about yourselves someday if you've done it all for yourself." I said a curt goodbye (my mother on the extension yelling, "Nancy! Nancy, don't hang up! Nancy, I'm going to call you back!"), and Andrew and I got down to figuring out how to do it ourselves.

In the end, we figured it out, and we bought that house. I guess Dad had a point. When I thanked him in his letter for "the ways in which you were hands-off," that was the incident of which I was thinking.

Especially given what happened to my dad six months after I wrote those words, I'm glad that I didn't take the opportunity to settle a score. Life is short and precious and unpredictable. When I closed the letter by telling Dad how much we appreciated his willingness to do whatever handyman tasks awaited him at our home, I didn't realize that he had already paid his final visit to our house. We still have unhung pictures and a door to a storage area that needs to be planed.

What are the things you value most about your parents, the lessons they've taught you, the gifts they have given to you and your family? What are the things you miss, or will miss, when your parents are gone?

Siblings

From the first time they tattled on us to the last time they offered advice around parenting concerns or career dilemmas, sibling relationships can be characterized by a mishmash of closeness and competition, of deep love and deep resentment. They are the people in our lives whom we're allowed to mock or excoriate mercilessly, but God forbid someone from the outside take a swing at them; our fury in that situation hath no bounds. For people who have no siblings, there is often a friend who is as close as a brother or a sister might be. (You can tell you have that type of person in your life if you adore them and are driven nuts by them in equal measure.)

Once I had polished off the letters to my parents, it made sense to write to the other two people who have known me since the day I was born: my older sister, Sally, and older brother, Larry. As adults, we're extremely close, even though they both live in Upstate New York and I'm in California. As kids, though . . . well, part of what went into my thank-you letter to Larry was a tiny diversion into heartfelt apology. It was for locking him in the basement one day when we were both in high school, for absolutely no other reason than he had gone down there to grab a soda from the wonky fridge that sometimes gave us an electric shock. Given that he was a 6'2" football player, I saw my moment for proactive retribution on someone whom I would never be able to best physically. (I can still hear him bellowing his plans for revenge through the basement window, as I cowered in exhilaration and terror at my neighbor Amy's house across the street.)

It was, in fact, reassuring to me as a parent to spend time thinking about some of the conflicts I'd had with my siblings over the years. Yes, we get along great now, but there had been healthy doses of really awful behavior toward one another as kids, which meant that there was hope for my daughters, who had their own occasional moments of mercilessness.

Sally has always been my parenting and career role model. A single mom to three kids by the time they were preteens, she worked full-time and simultaneously went back to school to pursue an entirely new career. I wrote to her:

When I brag about you to my friends, there are two things that top the list. The first is how you mothered your kids, who are three of my favorite people in the world. You set a parenting standard that I have tried to match, of affection and support tempered with judicious benign neglect, that resulted in three funny, kind, and capable people. That you did it largely on your own makes your achievement that much more impressive. I will be so proud and relieved if my own attempts to emulate that balance pay off with Maddy and Lucy.

It's been thrilling to see you find your second act via your passion for the travel and tourism industry. When I decided at age forty to get some business cards that said "Writer," I was absolutely thinking of how you pulled off your own big career change.

I also want to thank you for the way that you look after Mom, Dad, and Aunt Noonie. I know they appreciate the visits, calls, rides to doctor's appointments, muffins, roasts, and whatever else you provide them, but I want you to know that I do, too. You set such a good example of how to rove around in the world making it better for other people.

My siblings and I have drawn even closer since Dad died. The three of us now coordinate care for our mom like a well-oiled machine: Sally coordinates medical care; Larry picks Mom up for Sunday dinners; and I manage her finances. If there are vestiges of sibling rivalry or childhood resentments between us, they are buried under a mountain of gratitude for the support my siblings have given my parents, my kids, and me since we all moved out of Mom and Dad's house in the eighties.

By the way, I decided to include Larry's wife of twenty-nine years, Shelley, in my batch of sibling letters. Yes, she's an in-law, but that feels like a technicality. Or, as I wrote to her:

I'm also really grateful for the way you treat my mom and dad. You are so kind to them; you're like the best daughter they never had to go through the ugly teenage years with.

I know just as many people who have difficult relationships with their siblings as I do friends who are close to theirs, so this is another of those categories where it's worth taking time to think about how we're shaped by both positive and negative forces.

Perhaps you are the child who has had to take on more care of an aging parent, not necessarily due to choice, but rather due to a lack of involvement by your brothers and sisters. That can be an exhausting, expensive, and frustrating role to play on your own. But can you also envision a time in the future when that experience transforms into a gift for you, in the form of the knowledge that you honored your parents and set a good example for your own children? Or maybe you've been called to bail out a sibling from a problem of their own making, and maybe it has happened more than once. Could the validation of your strength and trustworthiness inherent whenever your siblings come to you for help be worth acknowledgment?

Maybe it is, maybe it isn't. I have a Pollyanna streak a mile wide, and I'm OK with your telling me that hard sibling relationships are simply that. Hard. But I hope you can find some sliver within that relationship for which to be grateful, even if it's just that once, your little sister baked you cookies for your birthday, or your older brother fixed a bike tire and taught you how to skateboard. Those were good moments to write down. You get to keep those with you, whether you decide to send the letter or not.

Grandparents

This is as good a place as any to mention that while writing these letters is meant to boost your happiness levels, and science suggests it will over the long haul, we don't necessarily get to pick which emotions we feel as we write them. I cried a few times as I thought about and wrote my letters—real sobby, ugly tears. In a few cases it came from the shame of acknowledging that I have not treated some people in my life as well as they deserved; in others, like letters to my late grandparents, it was grief when I allowed myself to feel the depth of what I had lost.

In fact, feeling anger, grief, or other negative emotions while you write your gratitude letters is probably a sign you are doing it right. When I asked Dr. Carter of the Greater Good Science Center if there were people for whom gratitude and happiness do not correlate, she said, "People can find gratitude hard because they're numb. They stay really busy, or they are on their devices all the time. Instead of feeling angry or anxious or sad or whatever the negative emotion is, they just pull out their phone and check their email and Facebook. It doesn't make that emotion go away; it just means we're not in touch with what we are feeling." She points out that people cannot selectively numb emotions. If you are uncomfortable sitting with feelings of anxiety or guilt or anger, you may not be able to feel gratitude, either, because the whole Emotion Factory is temporarily shut down while you play Candy Crush.

So, truly, it is OK and normal to shed some tears when you are writing these gratitude letters that are meant to make you happier. "It doesn't mean that you're going to be stuck in your grief; it means that you can sort of meet your grief where it is and see what's there," says Dr. Carter. On the other side of that tearful consideration is a full measure of what those people have brought into your life, a deep gratitude that can settle into your bones.

If your grandparents are still around to receive a letter, I would gently urge you to nudge their names northward in your list of recipients. Of course, a letter to a grandparent who played a critical role in your life but is no longer here to receive it would never be out of place. Maybe think of it as a memorial prayer, or good karma sent into the great beyond.

When my friend Melisa undertook her own gratitude-letter project, she found that the letters to her grandparents, who had been gone for decades by then, were some of her favorites to write. She told me, "My family, like so many others, has so many stories of these special family members that we repeat and laugh about when we're all together, but hunkering down by myself to write a letter about what they meant to *me* personally was an experience I treasure: it brought some things out of my long-term memory that I hadn't thought about in a while."

In her letter to her grandparents, Melisa wrote:

> It's been more than thirty-five years since you both passed, and I still miss you all the time. While I feel your presence a lot, I often wish you had lived to see me get married, earn my degree, and become a mother. I know that if you were still on this earth you would be my biggest fans, and I guess in some ways that knowledge is enough. I appreciate all that you gave to me, both the material and the non-tangible things, and hope that I am doing your legacy justice.

My maternal grandparents, who came from Yorkshire, England, gave me many gifts: an admiration of the royal family, an unbeatable recipe for Yorkshire pudding, and an inability to tolerate spices hotter than salt and pepper. I also credit them with my foundational belief in equality. Mine was not a family where a casual racial epithet would have been tolerated or excused, in any setting or for any reason. For that intolerance, I am grateful.

On my paternal grandparents' side, it would be a little trickier to articulate my gratitude, as I imagine it will be for everyone at some point as they work through their list. Grandma and Grandpa Davis moved from New York to North Carolina when I was a toddler, so we didn't see them as often as we did the Rochester grandparents.

When we did, there was a formality to their manner that freighted every visit with unspoken tension. I know they loved Sally, Larry, and me—I'm just not sure how much they liked us, especially as kids.

As an adult, I understand it a bit better—another situation when having a few more years under my belt made it easier to see a reason to write a thank-you letter. In North Carolina, my grandparents lived by a pristine little man-made lake ringed with azaleas. Grandpa golfed, and Grandma painted and was an avid birdwatcher. They had a ton of friends with whom they socialized. And they adored one another. When the Davis Five rolled up in the baby blue wood-panel station wagon, sticky from the two-day drive from Rochester and demanding to be fed and entertained, I'm sure they had a Dorothy Parker moment; i.e., "What fresh hell is this?"

Grandpa Davis died before I had time to form a more meaningful, adult relationship with him, though I will never forget his lectures on the virtues of bananas and their potassium. When I feel peckish and reach for a banana, that's Grandpa D at work.

But when I moved to Germany, Grandma Davis and I started writing letters to one another. She had visited the country with Grandpa years earlier and adored it, so I tried to share with her all the details of places I had gone and seen. She wrote me back frequently, voluminous, warm letters that I have kept wrapped with a ribbon. Through these letters, written when I was in my twenties and she was in her eighties, I was finally able to appreciate her in a way that had eluded me for years. So, I would include that detail—the happiness I felt every time I picked up my mail in Germany and saw a pastel envelope addressed to me in Grandma's rounded cursive and covered with stamps for overseas postage.

And, of course, without my grandparents, I wouldn't have the parents I adore. Which means I wouldn't be here, and neither would my beloved daughters. If the fact of your own existence is all you can be grateful for to someone who is on your list, that's still something.

Spouses/Partners

Remember how I said that your plans for this project might take a detour at some point, and that's OK? Here's where mine went sideways.

When I jotted down the preliminary list of names for my goal of fifty letters, I skipped down the spreadsheet to write names in rows 48, 49, and 50: Lucy, Maddy, and Andrew. My theory was that I would write the final thank-you letters to my children and husband as a sort of grand finale, the big fireworks at the end of the show. What a neat and graceful ending! How in control of things I am!

Then my dad died. And a cold panic set in that, after six months of writing, I hadn't even written the people I love the most to tell them I love them the most. What was I waiting for, when people we love can get snatched away in the space of half a season? As soon as the clouds of grief lifted enough to grant me the clarity to start writing my letters again, I started with Andrew and the girls.

At that point, Andrew and I had been married for twenty-four years. I'm pretty sure the last time I'd written him anything more substantial than a note on scrap paper that said, "Heading to the grocery store, text me if you need something," was once when we were new parents, almost twenty years earlier. I was furious about something, probably about what I saw as an imbalance of housework and childcare duties, so furious that I couldn't verbalize what I wanted to say. When I get upset, I move into the Sputter Zone, where I wave my hands a lot and rarely land a sensible point. But Andrew negotiates complex financial deals for a living—conflict is built into his day—so he goes quiet, calm, and logical. It is not an equal match-up. Rather than risk head-on confrontation, I decided to cover two sheets of notebook paper in handwriting with my raging complaints and leave it on his dresser. Love, Nan.

The fact that I can't even remember what I was mad about then is as good a reminder as any that, if you've been with someone for a long time, details start to blur. Specifics get lost in the passage of time. That's great if it takes the rough edges off a historical conflict, but unfortunately it's just as true for the wonderful things you want to remember.

I know for a fact that back when I was newly in love with Andrew at grad school in Arizona and we had to live apart for a semester, I fell asleep at night thinking of him. I missed him so much. I'd run the tape in my head on repeat of all the conversations and gestures that had captivated me, starting from the night we met in the on-campus pub, and I would think, "I never want to forget these moments."

Spoiler alert: I've forgotten some of those moments. I met

him at age twenty-four, and I'm fifty-three now, and I have more than double the amount of life experience to try to hold somewhere in my brain pan, not to mention passwords for approximately 534 websites. No amount of ginkgo biloba supplements can help the kind of forgetting that takes place on the daily around here.

So, taking a moment to memorialize the things for which I'm grateful to Andrew played at least three purposes: an expression of gratitude for him to read, a reminder to me of the reasons I am lucky to have him, and, for at least one page's worth of material, a bulwark against forgetting. As much as I can tell you today the exact things for which I'm grateful about Andrew, like his steadfast support when my father died, his devotion to our kids, and the fact that he cleans the girls' hair out of the shower drains so I don't have to, there's no guarantee that I'll remember those things five, ten, or another twenty-four years from now. Better to write it down.

There's another reason the letter to your spouse or partner can be so important in the modern era. You may not have a written record of your courtship, if it started after digital communication became the default. Although that semester apart back in 1991 was painful to endure, it did yield one rich benefit: snail mail. I was in Arizona, he was in New York, and the internet was but a glimmer in Al Gore's eye. We couldn't afford big, long-distance phone bills, and Andrew hates talking on the phone anyway. So, we wrote letters, and I still have every one that he sent me.

If you met your partner even a few years after I met mine, in the era when AOL discs came in the mail, you might not have that analog documentation of your relationship. Our kids certainly won't, likely not even emails that could be printed out. I imagine a conversation between Grandma and her granddaughter in 2070: "I still remember the first time I saw your granddad on Snapchat, before the message automatically deleted 15 seconds later. He'd chosen the Summer Barbecue filter." The granddaughter will nod, wondering why old people are so sentimental, and her brain chip will automatically transmit that thought into the neural network, at the end of which her boyfriend sits in his pod, gaming and taking Soylent Green through a feeding tube.

My point is, the physicality of this letter alone makes it worth writing.

Probably the biggest reason of all to write this is the human tendency to take the people we love the most for granted. If you're in a solid relationship, you know this. It's one of the main benefits. You don't thank your partner for every single thing, nor is it likely you expect articulations of gratitude from dawn to dusk for all you do. Most of the time, that's fine; we'd never get the laundry folded or finish reading a book if we had to vocalize our thanks for everything the person we've chosen to spend our life with has done for us, even on an average Tuesday. "Thanks for making the coffee/driving the carpool/paying the electric bill/watering the plants/including me on your company's health insurance even if I didn't need it today/flicking the lint off my sweater as you passed me in the hallway/boosting my credit rating/planning dinner/buying groceries for dinner/cooking dinner/cleaning up from dinner/planning tomorrow's dinner," etc.

But research has quantified a real impact of expressing exactly this type of day-to-day appreciation. In a 2010 study on the relationship between gratitude, indebtedness, and romantic relationships, researchers concluded that "gratitude was associated with increased relationship quality for both members of the couple. . . . The little things may make a big difference within the daily lives of individuals in romantic relationships. Gratitude may help to turn 'ordinary' moments into opportunities for relationship growth, even in the context of already close, communal relations."

We yearn to hear more gratitude from our partners. The 2012 John Templeton Foundation study found that 47 percent of women wish their spouse or partner would express more appreciation for what they do, and while six out of ten men think their partner or spouse expresses the right amount of appreciation, fewer than half of the women in the study felt that way. Here's another eye-popping stat from that survey: people are more likely to express gratitude to a waiter at a nice restaurant (58 percent of respondents) than to their spouse (49 percent). Yikes, garçon.

With this letter, you have a chance to not take things for granted. To show your partner that, yes, you still see them. You still choose them. And these are specific reasons why.

Is your partner your cheerleader? Is he/she kind to your parents and siblings? Does your partner hold you accountable in ways that you know benefit you? Are they devoted coaches of your children's sports teams? Do they perform miracles by stretching the grocery budget? The more specific you can be, the more the person you love will feel appreciated and recognized.

Way back in the mists of time, when I told Andrew I was thinking of writing letters to commemorate my fiftieth birthday and explained to him how I thought it might work, he immediately said, "DON'T WRITE ONE TO ME!" Who says that? Who in their right mind doesn't want a thank-you note? It made me laugh and laugh, and then I proceeded to ignore him and write him one anyway. It's possible I presented the finished letter to him with a celebratory "Ha HA!" while lifting my arms overhead in an outstretched victory sign and moonwalking. Et voilà, you now know the secret to our lengthy marriage: I married someone who still makes me laugh, and we have a healthy streak of contrarianism toward one another that keeps things jumping. That observation was in the letter.

Maybe someday when we're gone and Maddy and Lucy or our theoretical grandkids are wondering what made their parents or grandparents tick, my letter to Andrew will provide a helpful clue. (The thought of their reading it is, by the way, why I used secret code to thank Andrew for the other arena in which we keep things jumping. I'm a WASP-y prude from way back, and no one's kids need to be given that mental image of their parents.)

Despite saying he didn't want a letter, Andrew seemed genuinely pleased to read it. And I was genuinely pleased to have the pressure on my heart lifted, that after all those comforting years of taking each other for granted, I'd remembered to tell Andrew, really tell him, what he means to me now.

Children

I feel like there are two modes anchoring the ends of the spectrum of modern parent-child relationships. On one end is the worshipful parent who believes that every utterance from her children is prophetic, that each piece of macaroni art deserves a box frame from Michael's, and that each outgrown tube sock requires a proper grieving and burial.

On the other end are the people who seem really, really pissed that this whole "parenting" gig requires them to spend a lot of time with small children, who post their children's mistakes on social media to widen the circle of public derision, and who are counting down the days until these ungrateful bastards move out and they can get back to their real love: wine.

The rest of us lie somewhere on that spectrum, moving up and down depending on the barometric pressure, the sass factor, and how many times we must tell you to put that milk back into the refrigerator, anyway. We're neither, or both, attentive enough nor/and dismissive enough at any given moment. We're all imperfect, except in one way: we really do love our kids. That's what these letters can help remind our kids, and us. Our bonds with our children are unique—not even the relationship they have with a co-parent is the same as the one they have with you—and deserve momentary recognition and celebration.

Another reason to write these letters: the pace of life, especially if the kids are still living at home. I see you, Dad who is waking up early to drive Junior to hockey practice and then goes on to your entire workday before coming home again to help out with math homework and maybe, just maybe, if there's still time, watch half a Netflix special before you nod off. And you, Mom whose child has dropped the dreaded, "I think I'm supposed to bring brownies to Spanish class tomorrow," as you pulled her bedcovers up under her chin, so you're up early to get those in the oven while returning a work email and rejiggering your day to cover for the carpool because the other driver is sick today. You are seen. You are already flat out. You do not have a lot of time for anything, including letter writing. Especially letter writing.

But what if writing the letter could help make all the other flat-out stuff feel more worthwhile, more a privilege than a burden? When I wrote to Maddy and Lucy, it did feel like a chance to not just contemplate the size of the job I do for them, but the reasons that job enriches my own life. It gave me an excuse to think about the contours of the two little souls (I get that they're old enough to drive, but sometimes we still see the toddlers they were, right?) who will be connected to me for the rest of my days.

When we become parents, we lock into the day-to-day job responsibilities so fully that sometimes it's hard to put our heads above water and think about why we continue to do it. There are certain opportunities, like the kindergarten graduation when tiny children sing a sign-language version of "Somewhere Over the Rainbow," and you feel your heart will explode with joy and vulnerability and devotion and ohmigod they're now opening a construction paper butterfly they've made, and that's it, the parents are now sobbing too hard to press "record" on their phones, and the kids have to take it again from the top. Those moments are beautiful, and the memories stay with us (as does the imprint of the kindergarten-sized wooden chairs on our adult-sized behinds).

But by writing a letter, you're memorializing more than a single moment. And you're doing it in a way that can be reread and treasured and shared—both by the writer and by the recipient as that person grows up and, perhaps, becomes a parent themselves. That's probably worth taking thirty minutes out of your week, once, to create—isn't it?

I had a mini-lesson in this, and ironically it came from one of my kids. When Lucy was twelve, she called my parents and siblings and a few close friends and interviewed them on the topic of "Our Favorite Things About Nancy." She then transcribed their answers and put them into a photo album, along with a picture of me that she felt represented their thoughts. (For instance, "I love her sense of style" from my sister, Sally, is accompanied by a picture of Kate Middleton with a cutout of my face taped over hers. So creepy! So right.) It was an incredibly thoughtful gift. But a few months after Dad died, it became more than that.

Of my parents' three kids, I was the one who moved away, farther and farther. I went to school for international business, and by the time I was thirty I had lived in Vienna, Munich, Phoenix, Quebec City, and Washington, D.C., finally settling in Oakland, California, across the country from my parents. While I talked to my parents a couple of times a week throughout my adult life, distance and finances meant I only saw them three or four times a year. Sally and Larry and their families were the ones in their lives on a daily basis, present and helpful and connected to our parents in a way I, through my own choices, never could be.

After my dad died, this haunted me. Had I screwed up by being so far away from my parents for so many years? What had I lost by my persistent determination to head for bright lights and big cities? What level of closeness had I sacrificed?

One day a few months after Dad died, when feeling particularly low, I pulled out the little photo album Lucy had compiled for me and flipped to my dad's page. There, next to a picture of me taken on a trip to the North Island of New Zealand, she had documented my dad's response when asked to name his favorite thing about me: "I love how independent and adventurous she is." It still makes me cry to look at that page. Dad wasn't mad that I had such wanderlust. It was one of his favorite things about me. How kind of Lucy to commit that to paper so I could read it when I needed to—and how wonderful of you to consider doing that for your own children.

One thing I really loved about writing to my two kids was the chance to "see" them as individuals. Maybe it's because we have a boxed set, but since the day Lucy came home from the hospital, "Are you driving The Girls?" and "Where are The Girls?" and "What time do The Girls get home?" was always the shorthand for two people who are, in fact, vastly different, no matter how much they physically resemble one another.

What are the specific traits that each of your children, if you have more than one, brings to the family? How do they handle obstacles and opportunities? What have you learned from them? If it is hard to take that step back, think about how your friends and extended family would characterize your children. What do their teachers notice? What are their interests about which they've educated you? (Hello, parents who are now basically paleontologists/entomologists/baseball historians thanks to a child's interest in dinosaurs/bugs/Jackie Robinson.)

Here's how I framed it to Lucy, whose perseverance and determination will move mountains during her lifetime:

One of the things that I admire about you is your persistence and your resilience. Whether it's a mishap at a ballet audition, a coveted acting role that travel delays prevented you from trying out for, or a hard math or engineering concept, you just keep trying. You said to me recently that you think you are creative at trying different approaches until you find your way to an answer, and I want to tell you: never lose that self-awareness and confidence and creativity. It will take you so, so far. You inspire me to try and try again.

And here's part of what I wrote to Maddy, whose self-confidence and willingness to be true to her values has taught me to stick to mine:

Simply put, you know who you are, and you are true to yourself. I marvel at your confidence and your faith in yourself; as a writer I am sometimes—often?—filled with doubt about whether what I'm writing means anything to anyone, anyway. But I see you tackling your college workload with enthusiasm, and making friends with other smart, arty girls, and trying new things simply because they sound interesting. And I think, OK, I just need to have faith that I'm on the right path, and I need to put in the work, and I need to surround myself with the right people, like Maddy does, and I'm going to be just fine. So, thank you for being an inspiration to me.

I hope that, just as my dad's thoughts about my peripatetic lifestyle lifted me at a time I felt low, the letters I wrote The Girls (there I go again) will stand as a reminder to them when they need it of how loved they are, the strengths they possess, and the support they have. And as the writer of these letters, I have a reminder of the qualities of these amazing young people who will one day be in charge of deciding whether or not to commit me to Shady Pines Nursing Home, so that's reassuring.

One helpful hint on the kid letters: I don't know what the sibling dynamics are under your roof, but I recommend doling these out on the same day, even if you write them at different times. Why start a fight you can avoid? And of course, you want to make these generally the same length; only a rookie hands out ammunition for the "Dad loves me more than he loves you because I got eight paragraphs and you only got seven!" argument. Anyone who's counted Christmas presents at one in the morning on December 25 to make sure there's parity knows exactly what I'm talking about.

Finally, writing these letters—almost eight months after I'd started this whole project—was a good reminder that I did not control the reaction that people had to receiving them. Sure, some of the people to whom I'd written had by then acknowledged their letters in person with a big hug, via a phone call, or even by writing back, all of which was wonderful and gratifying. Others were more circumspect in their reactions, sending a brief thank-you text or making a quick mention when I next spoke to them.

Funny story: It took six months for my physical therapist friend Dawn to acknowledge the letter I wrote her, even though I saw her frequently during that time. I wondered about her silence, but told myself that maybe she just wasn't comfortable saying anything back. What turned out to be the reason for the delay? I had tucked her letter into the front cover of a book she had asked to borrow, and that's how long it took her to reach the bottom of the book pile on her coffee table. Boy, was she mortified when she finally cracked the cover.

Still, if you are writing thank-you letters to elicit a round of cheers directed back to you, take a breath, or a knee, or a tranquilizer. Your job is to express your gratitude for what the people in your life have done for you, and once you've done that, you're done. Any acknowledgment you get is gravy, and you have to be OK with that.

I say this because after I mailed Maddy's letter off to her at college, where she was enjoying her freshman year and taking, among others, a seminar class called "Pop and Protest," in which they discussed the political ramifications of Beyoncé's "Formation" video, it took her a few days to call once she had received it. Look, if I were getting graded on my knowledge of Beyoncé, I too would make that a priority.

As for Lucy, who was up to her neck in her sophomore year of high school and ballet rehearsals when I handed over her letter, she read it and thanked me. Then she got sucked back into the whirlwind that is life for a sixteen-year-old. When I saw the letter still sitting on the kitchen table a few days later, I moved it to her desk in her bedroom and can only assume that it is there still, somewhere in the pile of papers, to be discovered by anthropologists at some far future date. Or, better yet, by Lucy on a day she needs a reminder of how loved and appreciated she is.

The part you control about writing your thank-you letters ends when you sign them. After that, the universe takes over.

Extended Family Members

I became an aunt while I was in college, and it was a twofer; my nephews Zachary and Daniel were born within a week of each other. These boys, and the two younger siblings who were eventually added to each of their families, have added so much in my life—starting with tons of practice at diaper changing that came in handy when my own kids were born, and an unwavering determination to wait to have those kids until I was well and truly ready for the workload.

This is the part of the thank-you-note list where you get to ruminate on the people outside your immediate family who may share your nose, hair color, and propensity for eczema or flat feet. These letters are for the aunts and uncles and nieces and nephews and cousins who extend the reach of the word "family" to the far corners of your world. The Chinese side of Andrew's family simply refers to everyone as "cousin," and I've always liked the simplicity of that; it doesn't matter if you're once removed on your father's side, or a second cousin by way of Aunt Amina and Uncle Anton, whose grandparents were neighbors back in the old country. "Cousin" is as "cousin" does, and if there is someone in the family tree who has made a difference in your life, held you up, or taught you lessons, or has simply been part of the family traditions that keep you grounded, this might be a good time to let them know you appreciate it.

My extended-family list started with letters to my nieces

and nephews. I decided to tackle one family at a time, oldest to youngest kid; since they're all grown up now and out of their parents' houses I didn't send them on the same day, but that's something you might consider doing on behalf of family dynamics.

Being an aunt or uncle is a vastly underrated job. You get all the benefits of familiarity and closeness with the niece or nephew, but if you're lucky you can have enough objectivity and distance to be considered way, way cooler than their parents. Plus, you probably have a higher tolerance than their parents do for treating potato chips as a vegetable and buying that really annoying toy that, after all, you don't have to live with. No wonder these kids adore you.

Just as those letters to your own kids can point out and hold up behaviors that you understand are special and valuable, letters to your nieces and nephews give you a chance to think about the myriad ways your siblings' children have enriched your life. My nieces and nephews, all of whom grew up near each other, treat their much younger California cousins as part of the gang whenever they visit. They've never made my girls feel anything but welcome, especially during our annual summer sojourn to a family camp in the Adirondack Mountains. Here's how I put it to Sally's son, Daniel:

I am also forever grateful for the way you and your cousins made Maddy and Lucy feel like the luckiest youngest cousins ever. Nothing makes me happier than watching you guys interact at Family Camp; there's something special about that cousin relationship, especially the way you can pick up at exactly the spot you left off, no matter how much time has passed in between. I hope you guys will continue to have each other's back and stay in touch as everyone goes out into the big wide world. I can't think of a better cohort of people for my girls to be associated with.

And to my brother's daughter Shannon, who sometimes stayed with our kids when Andrew and I traveled:

I'm also exceedingly grateful for the kindness and affection you've always shown Lucy and Maddy. And when the rubber has hit the road (oooh, sorry, didn't mean to bring up that time when some mom backed into our car while you were parked and waiting for the kids in the school parking lot) you have REALLY been there for them, making it possible for Uncle Andrew and me to go off on a few adventures. It meant a lot to Andrew and me to have such a trustworthy young woman we could rely on for our kids so we could get away and really enjoy ourselves.

You get the picture. If you have them, each of your nieces and nephews brings a different hue to the family tapestry. These letters are a chance for you to thank them for what that means to you.

Special aunts and uncles get their letters in this section, too. For the same reasons you make a singular adult figure in your younger relatives' lives, perhaps your parents' siblings are especially important to you for the way they supported you while you were growing up. I have one aunt in particular who is a near-cult figure to my friends for the stories I've told about her over the years: my mom's oldest sister, Eunice, whom we call Noonie.

First, obviously, is the name. But my eldest aunt is more than just an ear-pleasing anachronistic nickname. She has been more like a third parent to Sally, Larry, and me over the years, with the attendant frustrations and tribulations. Noonie and her late husband, Pete, had that most righteous of features at their house when we were growing up in the seventies—an above-ground pool—and we spent entire summers floating in it, pruning up while we dove for little plastic discs called Plakies.

Noonie has always had a cozy relationship with the spiritual world and the absurd, believing equally in Sasquatch, messages from Beyond the Veil, and *National Enquirer* headline stories about UFOs. I'm pragmatic to the extreme, but Noonie is the reason I read my horoscope every day and don't dismiss it when someone says they've had a premonition. A few years ago, Sally and I drove our mom and Noonie for an overnight trip to Lilydale, a Spiritualist community in western New York. It is Noonie's favorite vacation spot, where basically every permanent resident is a psychic who gives readings to the visitors, and it was indeed a trip.

Here's how I put it:

Noonie, I can't tell you how lucky I feel to have you as my aunt. You have always treated me with such love and affection—I could become the worst person in the entire world, and I still feel like you would be happy to see me. That's a really nice feeling to be able to carry around with me every day.

I remember all the millions of summer days we spent in your backyard pool, running around the perimeter in circles to make whirlpools, diving for Plakies, and making fun of you, Mom, and Aunt Margaret as you "exercised" doing "water aerobics" that were never so rigorous as to interrupt your conversation. Then we would eat lunch at your picnic table until that fateful moment: "Nancy, go get ice pops for the kids." It was only the promise of the gustatory rush of pure artificial coloring and sugar that made me brave enough to open your freezer door, holding an arm out to deflect all the pies and ice cream and whatnot that had just been waiting to fall out onto an unsuspecting victim.

You've always been sweet to Andrew, and I appreciate that too. I love that when the girls were born, you had their astrological charts done for them. I don't know if they're living up to or down to the potential that the stars held, but I do know that they love to come see you when they visit Rochester. I'm glad that even though you don't see each other often, you still share a connection.

I'm so glad we finally got to go to Lilydale together last summer. I totally understand why it's such a special place to you; not only is it lovely, but there was a weirdly soothing energy about it that made me want to go back, too. I'll keep fingers crossed that we can make another pilgrimage soon.

One final thing: you are the only person who still asks me when I am going to move back to Rochester. I've been away for almost thirty years, and the odds of my returning aren't high. But I love that you ask me the question.

What are the ways that your aunts and uncles have brought love, support, and joy into your life over the years? What lessons have they taught you, from what scrapes have they helped extract you (perhaps without your parents even knowing), what are the ways they have lent a listening ear, an open wallet, or a helping hand over the years? Since my dad passed away, his brother, Ray, has been a source of reassurance, facts, and details when we needed to fill in the blanks doing the inevitable administrative tasks related to tying up all the loose ends when someone dies. Without Uncle Ray's knowledge of my dad's whole history, we would have struggled. That he relays it to us over the phone in a voice strikingly similar to my late father's is a gift both painful and beautiful.

And my periodic gentle nag: if you have aging parents, chances are that your aunts and uncles are also getting up in years. Noonie turned ninety last year, and I don't know how much longer I'll have the chance to hear her awesome signature signoff when we've finished up a phone call: "Call me soon, but if you see Sasquatch, call me right away." If it makes sense to push aunts and uncles higher on your list to get these letters into their hands sooner, that would never be a bad decision.

And don't forget all those cousins, however you define the term. Whether just a few or an entire battalion, you may have grown up with a group of kids who share grandparents and memories of the same family traditions at holiday parties and barbecues that wove you into a comprehensive unit. These letters are a nice chance to think about the ways your cousins have helped memorialize and institutionalize your understanding of the bonds and the reach of family.

There's real value in taking the time to reinforce the ties you share with people who have the same surname or genetic code as you. And hey, if you do it right, you might even get first dibs on the potato salad at the next family reunion.

In-Laws

This is where you get a chance to shake the branches of another family tree and see what treasures fall out: that of the person with whom you're partnered.

Now, I'm not going to suggest for a minute that in-law relationships aren't tricky. How tricky? In a 2012 study led by sociologist Terri Orbuch at Oakland University in Michigan that examined the links between emotional ties to participants' birth families and their in-laws during the first year of marriage and marital stability over the first sixteen years of marriage, researchers found that having close ties to your in-laws in the first year of your marriage can either help or hurt your marriage, depending on your race and gender. A 2015 study that looked at "hurtful mother-in-law messages" found that marital quality for a daughter-in-law and her husband depended on whether they both interpreted Mom's message the same way, and also on whether the daughter-in-law believed her mother-in-law's hurtful message was motivated by internal or external factors. Acres of space for misunderstanding! Fabulous.

The point is, you may have married or partnered your way into the best family in the world, and there is just some awkwardness and vulnerability built in to those relationships; you're not imagining it. Your partner's family basically said, "Be careful out there among them English," and look what he/she dragged back inside the family compound. Hollywood gets it: you have all seen 3,421 movies and television shows where the in-laws are awful, and that's not even counting *Monster-in-Law*, in which Jane Fonda and Jennifer Lopez tussle over Michael Vartan, culminating in an improbable slap-fight where everyone's hair and makeup remain impeccable. Even if (spoiler alert!) that movie has a happy ending—like Michael Vartan was going to let J. Lo slip through his fingers—we're primed with the message that in-law relationships are fraught with opportunities for raw emotions and hurt feelings.

And that's for in-law relationships that are still intact.

Statistically speaking, pretty much every one of us has been touched by divorce somewhere along the way—our parents', our own, that of our siblings, or that of our children. Expecting you to consider writing a thank-you letter to someone with whom you or a family member is no longer connected is what my dad would have termed "an awful damn lot." So, if you need to take a big exhale and turn the page to think of someone else who deserves a letter, I get that.

But before you do, let me remind you that these letters are all about homing in on the good in our relationships, the small specific gifts we've been given to help us get to where we are today. Maybe your ex-sister-in-law shook your brother's self-esteem, but before the marriage ended she taught you how to knit, and now that's your favorite way to de-stress. Or your ex-father-in-law helped make your former marriage rough terrain but remains devoted to your children.

Instead of focusing on the ways your in-laws (outlaws?) may

fall short, you could use your letter to thank them for the things they do for which you really are grateful. In management, in parenting, in training dolphins or dogs, the carrot approach is legitimate: praise the good behavior to see more of it. You can acknowledge the good without excusing the bad, and let me go back to the drumbeat: you don't need to send every letter.

Interesting fact about my in-laws: most of them came along with me on my second date with their son/brother.

Andrew and I went out for the first time, and then four days later he was due to graduate from our school in Arizona. After only one date and even knowing he was about to leave town, I was pretty sure I had met my future husband. I'm not rash—I did think a second date was in order before I started shopping for a veil. But because of exam schedules, the next time we saw one another was the night before his graduation. His family had just arrived in town to watch him get his diploma. "Come for dinner to my apartment and meet my family," he said in a message he left on my answering machine.

As I listened to the message, I crumpled to my knees in the bedroom of my apartment. Come for dinner? The boyfriend before this had made me wait a full two years before introducing me to his family. OH, I'M A'COMING FOR DINNER ALRIGHT!

When I walked into Andrew's off-campus apartment that night, the first person I saw was my future father-in-law, BT, standing in the kitchen cooking a ginormous pan of fried rice. He had a gorgeous shock of thick white hair, and my two thoughts, in order, were, *Andrew will keep his hair!* (true!) and *Andrew must love to cook, too!* (false!). My mother-in-law-to-be, Helen, and Andrew's sister, Suzanne, were also there, friendly and kind even though I'm guessing they had learned of my existence about fifteen minutes earlier, or perhaps when they heard my knock at the door. Over the course of dinner that night, listening to the easy and affectionate way Andrew and his parents and sister bantered with one another, I thought, *Yup, I can work with this.* I would not be so presumptuous as to suggest which anecdotes belong in any gratitude letters my husband might choose to write in his life. I am saying that my in-laws totally closed the sale for Andrew that night.

When I wrote a letter to my mother-in-law, Helen, I wanted to thank her for two important things she has brought to my life: devotion to our kids, and inspiration to stay engaged as I age:

> As a grandma, of course, you are wonderful. I know it's hard that you and the girls live so far apart, but there's never been a time when they doubted your devotion or admiration for their feats (and ballet feets). I think it's a big part of why they are growing up to be such loving people. So, thank you for your efforts in the common cause.
>
> I also admire your zest for involvement—wherever you go, you seem to create community and connections, in ways that are often entertaining other people! I feel like all those choirs you've sung in, those music performances you've organized, and those variety nights you've facilitated have brought joy to the audience and reminded us all of the trained performer you are.

A few weeks later, when I wrote to my sister-in-law, Suzanne, I thanked her for being so involved with Maddy and Lucy's lives here in Oakland, even though she lives in Austin. Little did I know how her loving generosity toward her nieces would manifest after I sent the letter. When my father died, Lucy happened to be spending five weeks at the University of Texas Austin at a summer ballet intensive program. It was Aunt Suzy and her boyfriend who raced over to campus to comfort our daughter over the sad news in the hours that followed, calling us to reassure us that they would watch out for her. If I had a do-over on the letter I wrote Suzanne, that anecdote would be front and center.

My experience in writing was that, particularly in delicate relationships like those we may have with our in-laws, the gratitude letters have real utility as a means of focusing on what works well. Next time you toil over Thanksgiving dinner and someone sighs, "You put maple syrup on your sweet potatoes? That's gross," you might excuse yourself to flip to that person's letter in your Thank-You Project file instead of threatening them with the blunt edge of a butter knife.

And if there is nothing else for which to thank your in-laws, try this: they were the fire in which the partner you love was forged. That's already a lot.

Not-Related-by-Blood Family

A final word as we come to the end of the people in your family to whom you may want to send a letter: no one says family must be defined by genetics.

While the categories I've outlined above all follow the traditional classifications of family, we thankfully live in a time when any given person's definition of family may be much broader. Maybe your family tree is more like a quaking aspen, which grows in a forest of single trees, all with an interconnected underground root system.

I would venture to say that if you are someone who has deliberately created a support network of not-related-by-blood family, you may have even more to be thankful for than the average bear. Something drove you to identify and cast your lot with the members of your chosen family, and something in them makes you treasure their presence in your life. Those people deserve to know.

Godchildren. Foster parents. The not-related "grandma" who never forgets your birthday or one of your sporting events, the father figure who taught you to shave and tie a proper Windsor knot after your own dad disappeared, your child's friend who basically lives in your home and looks to you for parental mooring because her own family is in disarray—you may not share DNA, but that has scant bearing on whether you're family or not.

In fact, I'll even go out on a limb here (get it?) and encourage you to include pets on this part of the list. A lot of us have gained more comfort and understanding from the four-legged/feathered/reptilian creatures in our lives than we have from the ones who walk upright, have a credit rating, and carry a cell phone. If you've been helped, shaped, or inspired by the animals in your life, you could write about that.

Thanks to my brother Larry, who was basically an underage Marlin Perkins, I grew up in a house full of dogs, lizards, gerbils, fish, turtles, and an iguana named Spike. But the pet of my life was a German shorthaired pointer named Achilles, whom we adopted when the girls were five and eight, and with whom we got to spend eight excellent years. I adored him.

If you know the breed, you know they have two speeds: spastic motion and Velcro'd to their owner's leg. Every single day we had him, Achilles made sure I was up and out of my chair for a big midday walk, rather than hunched over my desk writing and courting spinal pain. He greeted my every appearance in a room like he was the prepubescent president of the Nancy Davis Kho Fan Club, complete with hyperventilation and tripping over his own feet in excitement. He drove me batty with his occasional need to eat grass in the front yard for an hour at two a.m., his counter-surfing thievery that claimed both an entire chicken and an entire corned beef, and his insistence on being exactly where I was trying to go, 0.03 seconds before I got there.

But that dog loved me with a purity and intensity that still makes me tear up a little to think about, even three years after he died. He made me much less scared of dogs that I encounter on the street, better at reading their body language and reacting appropriately. He welcomed every new person he encountered with a friendliness and openness that I would do well to emulate. Finally, he was a dream childhood pet for our daughters: gentle, goofy, and devoted. Maddy and Lucy will always have good memories of growing up alongside his sweet, furry self. Those are all things I would thank Achilles for if I were to write him a letter. And if he were still around, I'd read it aloud to him.

Who knows? I might sound to him like the "wah wah wah wah" teacher from Charlie Brown.

But something tells me Achilles would have understood every word.

FAMILY FIRST

 A

Won't Give In— Finn Brothers
Murder in the City—
    The Avett Brothers
We're a Happy Family—
    The Ramones
Family Affair—
    Sly and the Family Stone
Dear Mama—2 Pac
Mama, I'm Coming Home—
    Ozzy Osbourne

 B

Dance with My Father—
    Luther Vandross
Keep It Together—Madonna
One for Sorrow—Jeffrey Foucault
The Mother—Brandi Carlile
Father and Daughter—Paul Simon
Cousins—Vampire Weekend
Song for Eva Mae—Frank Turner
Ben—Michael Jackson
Me & My Dog—boygenius

CHAPTER 3

FEELINGS FOR FRIENDS

*Friendship is the only cement that
will ever hold the world together.*

—WOODROW WILSON

Up until this point in your list of letters, you've focused on the people to whom the universe saw fit to assign you, like some cosmic Sorting Hat game. Or, as my mom used to say when she heard me grousing about perceived mistreatment from her and Dad or one of my siblings, "If we could choose our families, we'd all be orphaned only children." Some people lucked out with their families, some didn't, but when it comes to friends, we finally get to exert some control.

Even as I was writing letters to family members, I knew there were people in my friend sphere who know me better than some of my blood relations do. They've been there through good times and bad, not from familial duty but because they chose to stay. To cop a phrase from Sally Field, your friends really, really like you. Sit for a moment with the grace of that fact.

In her book *Life Reimagined: The Science, Art, and Opportunity of Midlife,* journalist Barbara Bradley Haggerty described a fascinating experiment in which she participated that quantified the power boost that we get from our closest friends. It was conducted by psychology professor James Coan in the University of Virginia's Affective Neuroscience Laboratory. The experiment sounds like a fraternity hazing ritual gone awry: subjects lay in a brain scanner with an electric-shock cuff on their ankle, and the scanner tracked how the fear center of the brain—the hypothalamus—lit up whenever participants saw an image flash that signaled they had a 20 percent chance of receiving a mild shock in the next few seconds. (When I interviewed Barbara on my podcast about the experience, she assured me that "mild" was a vast understatement.)

The researchers tested subjects in three different states: alone in the scanner, holding the hand of a stranger, and holding the hand of someone with whom they shared a close relationship. When the subject was alone in the scanner, the hypothalamus/fear center lit up like a Christmas tree when that threat-of-shock image flashed; when the subject held the hand of a stranger and saw the same image flash, fear levels were somewhat subdued.

But when the subject held the hand of a close friend and that threat-of-shock image flashed, the fear center barely flickered. Why? Characterizing the study in a *UVAToday* interview, Dr. Coan said, "What we are finding here is that if our relationship is good and we are with someone we trust, we can say, 'Hypothalamus, you don't have to work as hard right now. Yeah, there is a threat, but chill out—the threat is not as threatening as if you were alone.' Your friend will help you deal with that threat; therefore, you can work less hard to deal with it, and that savings will keep you healthier in the long run." He added, "Having that hand to hold signals that you have resources—you have safety—so any particular stressor is just not as stressful as it might have been."

Writing a gratitude letter to the friends who have enriched your life along the way is an excellent means of ensuring that when you face a real-life threat, you will always have that metaphorical hand to hold.

Our friendships come in so many varieties—the BFF treasures, the friendships that stretch back to childhood, the ones that have popped up in our adult lives through work or school or our children. When you're deciding who belongs in this section, you may even pass over the terrain of friendships that are no more, the ones that burned hot enough to mold you in some important way but couldn't sustain for the long haul. Even if you don't send those letters, those were people who once mattered to you on the road to where you are today. That counts.

Best Friends

It's pretty easy to figure out who belongs at the top of the list of recipients of your gratitude letters to friends: start with the people to whom you've said, "Can you look at this weird bump on the back of my thigh and describe it for me?" Or the ones who have stared you deep in the eye and said, "I love you, but this haircut is not doing you any favors." Or the ones to whom you've turned for support when you have bad news and realized that they're more upset than you are, because not only is there bad news, but it is happening to someone they adore.

At the top of my list of friend letters was the very first person I spoke to on my college campus freshman year. I was all cock-eyed eighties optimism with my asymmetrical bob, my Madonna bracelets, and the finest-looking baggies that Limited had on offer that summer. *This is where my years working as a camp counselor have been perfect training,* I thought. *I know how to start a conversation with anyone!*

"HI, I'M NANCY! I LIVE ON THIS FLOOR OF LEIDY HALL. WHAT'S YOUR NAME?" I brayed to a petite blonde carrying an armful of clothes as she walked past me up a staircase.

Her eyes widened. "Maria," she said quietly, barely breaking stride.

I blushed and fled into my new dorm room, thinking, *Oh my god, what is WRONG with me? Why am I so uncool?! I scared that girl away!* Maria, it turns out, was in her room directly overhead, having exactly the same conversation with herself.

We were made for one another.

In the thirty-five years since that first meeting, we've applied straight hydrogen peroxide to each other's hair, vetted one another's husbands, watched each other's kids for an hour or for a weekend. At one point, when Maria and her husband, Ted, were moving houses in the Bay Area and had a two-week gap between homes, they and their three kids moved in with us temporarily. Suddenly, my housework was halved since she split it with me, and the conversation at the weekday dinner table was doubled since we had fresh voices and fresh topics. A decade later, Maria and I still refer to those two weeks as "The

Good Times" and wonder if buying a two-family compound might have been the way to go.

In keeping with Dr. Coan's research on the comfort and strength we receive from our friends, there were two occasions I wanted to memorialize in the letter I wrote to Maria:

> If I had to pick my most stupendous memory, I think it would be seeing you walk into the delivery room on Christmas Day 2000 as I was exhausted and in pain and thinking, *OK, Maria is here, I can do this.* That you were in the room when Lucy was born an hour later was a blessing beyond measure. And getting to be present in the delivery room with you when Ethan made his grand entrance to the world was one of the most humbling, fascinating moments of my life too. Thank you for letting me be a part of that.

It's one of the ironic challenges of the letters you write to your BFFs: you may have so much source material here that it can be tricky to narrow down the really important aspects of the friendship. For these wonderful people, you could probably fill eight sides of notebook paper, college-ruled, with sentences that start "How about the time that we . . . ?"

That's not necessarily a bad thing, of course. But this is where I'll challenge you to think hard about the precise gifts that your BFFs give you and what they've brought to your life that without them you might lack.

For instance, when Andrew and I moved to California for his job, we started a holiday tradition. We would share Christmas Eve dinner at Maria and Ted's house, and Christmas Day brunch at ours. When our little Christmas Day baby was born in 2000 and we asked Maria and Ted to be Lucy's godparents, spending December 25 together took on even deeper significance for our two families.

Maria helped me create new family traditions that are as precious to my daughters as any they were missing out on by being raised so far from their grandparents, aunts and uncles, and cousins. In this case, it isn't over the river and through the woods to Grandmother's house, but rather over the Oakland hills and through the Caldecott Tunnel to Maria and Ted's house. My gratitude for that tradition went in the letter.

Figuring out and cogitating on the support that came from my closest friends was one of my very favorite parts of this entire project. Writing a gratitude letter about people whom you may have long ago lumped into the friend zone gives you a reason to open and reexamine a treasure trove of memories.

After I finished Maria's letter, I set to spending a week thinking about my friend Jill, another dear friend from college who also lives in Oakland now. I realized the friendship I share with her is very different—complementary, maybe—to the one I share with Maria. Jill and I used to work in the same business field and both still do consulting in that arena, so she's always been a sounding board for things like project proposals, billable rates, and networking. We both do creative work now—hers in design, mine in writing—and she understands the tightrope challenge that is negotiating corporate versus creative endeavors. Our weekly hike together in the Oakland hills triples as a pep talk, a peer mentoring session, and an excuse to carbo load.

Jill's ability to empathize is extraordinary. And I knew the exact two actions of hers that made me realize it:

If I had to pick a moment that exemplifies to me the kind of friend you are, it would be when Lucy was a newborn and hospitalized for a week with a respiratory virus. I was terrified, frantic, sad in a thousand different directions as I stayed with her in the hospital around the clock. And then one morning you walked in with a giant hot latte, a box of chocolates, and a *Vogue* magazine. You made the handoff, stayed for just a few minutes—which was about all the company I was capable of handling in that moment—and left. Years later, when my beloved Achilles died, you dropped off a noodle kugel that allowed me to eat 19,000 calories of my grief. Your giant heart never ceases to amaze me and reminds me that I'm lucky to be in your circle.

When you think about your closest friends, consider the most important ways they have impacted you and try to get that onto the page. Do they cheer on your accomplishments and push you to follow your dreams and ambitions? Do they listen without judgment when you need a sounding board? Do they recognize before you do that you are running out of steam and need a break—a night out, a quiet walk, a predictable rom-com at the movie theater complete with a bottomless bucket of buttered popcorn? And then do they nag you until you make it happen?

Once you've written these letters, you may even find it easier to know which friend to lean on for a particular need in your life. As someone who has always held unreasonably high expectations of the people around me, I have learned a hard lesson in my fifty-plus years: no one friend can be all things for you. There is bound to be an arena where they fall short. Maria and Jill are always game for going on a hike with me, but going out in the city for a night of sweaty dancing and a late-night taco-truck run? Not so much. But it's OK because, I realized as I wrote my letter to her, that's what Dawn is for.

Another unexpected discovery from this group of letters was how surprised the recipients were to receive them. Much like with a longtime spouse, we tend not to tell our closest friends enough how lucky we are to have them in our lives. Why thank the air that keeps you breathing?

But science tells us there are good reasons to write them. In a 2017 article from the Greater Good Science Center, researchers Eric Pederson and Debra Lieberman wrote, "When we express gratitude to someone, we are effectively signaling that, by virtue of their actions, we value them more than we did before—and that we might be more likely to provide benefits to them in the future." They went on to say, "Hearing gratitude from someone might make us value her more, to the extent that we care about how our actions affect her.... This is because, out of the sea of people in the world, this person has indicated that she values us and is thus more likely to be an ally. Therefore, helping this person in the future might have a better chance of bolstering a new, beneficial relationship than helping others who haven't demonstrated that they value us."

In other words, you think you have a close, cooperative relationship with your best friends now? Wait until you send them their thank-you letters.

Childhood Friends

The first batch of friend letters I wrote were for people who, for the most part, I talk to frequently and are a presence in my daily life. But after sending those, I knew there were a few people who knew me in my most malleable, suggestible form to whom I owed a debt of thanks. People I hung out with when I was a dues-paying member of the Melissa Sue Anderson Fan Club and planning my Hollie Hobbie–themed tenth birthday: my childhood buddies.

Perhaps even more than the friends you make when you're older and more fully formed, childhood friends can play an oversize part in shaping the person you have become. They were in band with you when you discovered your love of performing, or in math class when you realized you were a writer. They were there as you tried on the various phases of adolescence and, through their feedback, helped you figure out which one(s) fit best. They were the sole other member of the middle school club you formed to discuss *Star Trek* (the original, obviously). They provided the corroborating alibi when you missed curfew because you didn't want to leave that one party. These friends bore witness to all the self-discovery that goes on between birth and age I-am-no-longer-on-my-parents'-dime.

Beyond the unmistakable emotional benefits of those childhood friendships, research has shown that there are long-lasting health benefits for which you might thank your playground friends. In a 2018 study published in *Psychological Science,* adult men who were reported by their parents to have spent lots of time with friends during childhood and adolescence evidenced lower blood pressure and obesity levels almost twenty years later. The researchers wrote, "These results provide strong evidence that integration with peers early in life is associated with physical health in adulthood, in particular risk for hypertension and obesity." So, if your doctor recently gave you an A+ on your annual physical, you could start your letter with thanks for that.

Given that I was writing these letters during a year in which I lost one of my parents, I realized there was something else childhood friends give us that is particularly meaningful: memories of our parents in their younger years. I know that when my high school friend Lisa pictures my dad, she sees the dark-haired Kodak engineer who was forever tinkering in his garage workshop on some home repair project. In return, I will always remember Lisa's late dad, Al, sitting at his kitchen table behind his newspaper, surrounded by three chatterbox teenage daughters and one chatterbox friend named Nancy, smiling through the cacophony with remarkable equanimity.

There's something tremendously comforting in knowing that your childhood friends see the entirety of the parent you've lost, just like you do.

The people on this part of the list may also have been present during (mis)adventures of your youth that stand out as meaningful. Or, as I wrote to my audacious friend Kitty, whom I met in first grade and remain close with even now that she lives in Australia:

You have always been someone in whose gentle soul and quiet demeanor lurks an adventurous, fun-loving friend— ready for anything and full of ideas. I would say that, when it comes to stories of my life that I still can't tell my parents, you figure in >50 percent of them.

No more details than that, sorry. I want my mom to read this book.

This group of letters may memorialize friendships that have lasted for decades. Maybe that's why in some of what I wrote to childhood friends, I had to acknowledge that the friendships had weathered a few bumps in the road. I've known Lisa for almost forty years, Kitty for almost fifty. In both cases there were periods of distance between us, and in both cases whatever made the friendship worthwhile eventually overcame the ill feelings. Here's how I put it in one letter:

Looking back at all the many, many years that have passed since we met, I want to acknowledge that our friendship has been tested and stretched and yet always bounces back to the original form. I think it's a testament to the durability and strength of what's there, and probably also the forgiveness and acceptance that comes with getting older. Honestly, I don't even know why we ever grew apart at ANY point, in part because my memory is going down the crapper.

Given the occasional viciousness of adolescence, one way to identify people to whom you owe thanks from this phase of life could be thinking of the kids who had your back when times were hard, when you were cut from a team or flunked a class, or when a bully set her targets on you.

Depending on the outcome of your situation and what it

taught you, you might even want to write a letter to that child-hood bully. If we are talking about people who have influenced our lives, I could have included a Mean Girl named Courtney on my list. She made my life hell in fourth grade, to the point that I begged my parents daily to let me transfer to a different school. What I would have written is that as a mom, I talked early and often to my kids about bullying behavior—how to identify it, how to react to it, and, most of all, how to never, ever be its perpe-trator. Her mistreatment of me when we were children made it easier for me to guide my own kids through that stage, which was something for which to be grateful.

But screw her. On reflection, I didn't want to give Courtney one more second of headspace than she'd already stolen from my life. Back to my *nice* childhood friends.

A last word about these letters to childhood friends. Maybe you were that exemplary eleven-year-old who loved writing thank-you notes and properly expressing gratitude for every kind thing done for you. Not me. I was super busy practicing my Dorothy Hamill skating moves on our next-door neighbor's backyard ice rink and conspiring to meet Andy Gibb.

So, think of this batch of letters as a way of properly express-ing gratitude from a grown-up perspective. As a kid, you may not have understood the significance of that friend who shared her lunch with you when yours didn't stretch quite far enough, or who tutored you after school so you wouldn't fall behind in class, or who insisted you enter a dance arm in arm with him when your original date backed out and left you standing there in a pink dress of your own design (Duckie, we love you. Blane, do better). But as a grown-up, you get it. Here's your chance to say so.

Hang-in-There Friends

There's a feature of childhood friendships that gets taken for granted right up until the day you graduate high school or college: time. At school, at sports and clubs, in your faith community, wherever you go as a kid, your friends are probably there too, giving you the luxury of long conversations and shared experiences. I, for instance, spent the entirety of the summer of 1977 sitting in the branches of a white poplar tree trading Wacky Pack cards and chewing Bubble Yum with my next-door neighbor, Mary Beth.

When you're a grown-up? Not so much. Once we're out in the work world and/or raising a family, demands on our time make it exponentially harder to meet people with shared interests and to put in the work it takes to nurture and sustain friendships. Which makes the friends who we meet in the regular course of our adult lives and who hang in there as real friends over time a special sort of precious.

These are the people we met at work, at the school playground, or down the hall when we moved into our first apartments. They remember our tyrannical first bosses and the anemic paychecks. They were co-chaperones for that awful rainy school camping trip that we survived only by laughing through our exhaustion (and carefully camouflaging a flask). They cried with us when the cat who was really our first baby passed away.

If you have children, you may have felt jubilation when you found yourself among fellow parents at preschool or kindergarten or soccer practice. After the relatively isolating experience that can be life with a newborn, just rubbing shoulders with people who *also* haven't slept well in three years or who *also* carry a purse that is 90 percent full of other people's belongings can feel exhilarating. *They get me,* you may think to yourself as you extricate a dirt-covered cookie out of your crying toddler's hand, surrounded by parents doing some variation of the same ritual. *These are my people.*

When Maddy started kindergarten, her elementary school's practice was to have families gather in a little kindergarten-only playground area for a few minutes before the first bell. The kids would play together until Ms. Treese emerged from the classroom, at which point the children were supposed to line up like cheerful ducklings and follow her in. The whole point was to make the transition easier on the kids. It gave us time to get to know fellow parents in the process.

Andrew and I very quickly became known as "The Heismans." As in, to get Maddy into the door of the classroom, you'd have to sort of cram her toward the door with one hand while turning your body to flee to the parking lot, much like the posture of football's Heisman Memorial Trophy. Maddy was *not* having this school nonsense and much preferred to follow her parents back to the car, for weeks. (She got over it. Parents of clingy kids: hang in there.)

It was an awful phase of parenting, to scurry away from our child to the receding soundtrack of her shrieks of indignation at being left behind. It left a couple scars. But the silver lining was that we bonded over it with a big group of sympathetic parents whom I was genuinely happy to see at the never-ending stream of parent nights, classroom parties, and field trips.

Then middle school arrived, the kids did more activities more independently, and it dawned on me: there were some people in my circle of friends who were merely convenient. They were perfectly nice, but we didn't have much in common besides the kids. If you took the kids out of the equation, it was hard to sustain a coffee conversation, let alone a friendship.

By the time the end of high school rolled around, I'd winnowed down those kindergarten friendships to a small handful of women whom, I knew, I'd have been friends with whether our kids were buddies or not. (And in many cases the kids spent much less time together than their moms did.) Having raised our kids together was merely one of many layers of the friendships I'd built with these ladies. I still wave to all those nice kindergarten moms and dads when I see them around town, but the women to whom I wrote thank-you letters are the ones with whom I plan to squander my Empty Nest years.

This notion of focusing on the quality, not quantity, of friendships as you get older has some scientific basis. A 2015 article from the Greater Good Science Center summarized a longitudinal study led by Cheryl Carmichael of Brooklyn College that looked at the mental health and social relations of participants. Researchers found that "the best outcomes in your 50s were associated with having had lots of social activity in your undergraduate years, and then focusing on some good, close friends as you started to reach your 30s."

One of my good, close people is Maureen, a Jersey girl and Bruce Springsteen fan. She has unapologetically and successfully pursued a career in fashion while raising her twins, in a way I find inspiring.

Maureen, I remember meeting you back on the kindergarten playground at the kids' elementary school—I categorized you as The Sporty Mom, what with the marathon you were training for. Little did I know how many other interests and talents lay in wait for me to discover as the years rolled past. Fashionista, traveler, reader, music fan, and—my favorite thing about you—down to earth East Coaster, an oasis of "don't fuck with me" Jersey attitude here in our sea of avocados and sage sticks. I love living in the Bay Area, but man, sometimes I need to hang out with a friend who doesn't confuse directness with rudeness. And, of course, I'm a latecomer to the Bruce fan club, but you've never held that against me.

There is another aspect of our friendship that I'm appreciative of—the fact that you take your career and your own life, independent of the kids, seriously, and don't apologize for it. There have been moments when I feel kind of bad because I do want to be a great writer and achieve something with it, and that means a lot of time and effort that I suppose I could have redirected to Maddy and Lucy (whether they wanted me to or not). But I could always look to you as an example of someone who embarked upon a whole new career once her kids started school and parlayed it into a thriving business with happy, long-term clients, and STILL had kids who turned out great. It gave me a lot of reassurance that it was OK to want to raise independent kids, a message that seems to get buried too easily these days.

I knew that when I wrote the letter to my friend Glynis, it needed to include her 2008 invitation to Maddy and Lucy to

"come on down to my daughters' ballet studio and just try it out!"
Her twin girls have long since quit ballet, and every year during
Nutcracker season when I am being driven insane by the never-
ending loop of Tchaikovsky, I send her texts threatening to end
the friendship and/or make her pay ballet-school tuition. But
I'm not really mad.

> I know I tease you about this a lot, especially on a certain
> weekend in December, but your invitation to Maddy and
> Lucy to have them try out a ballet class as guests of your
> daughters caused a seismic shift in their lives and ours, one
> that introduced them to what turned out to be the central
> joy of their young lives. I really can't thank you enough for
> being our entrée into that world, because the creative gift
> and outlet it has given our kids is beyond value. I am so
> grateful to your whole family for that.

The irony is that once her daughters and Maddy left for
college, Glynis and I started going to a hip-hop class together
on Saturday mornings. So, we are devoted dancers in our own
right, although what we're really devoted to is our post-class
ritual of a fat slice of pastry with a side of gossip at the pie shop
down the street from the hip-hop studio.

Again, these letters are a chance to remind yourself of the
specific gifts you've been given from these relationships and to
express to your friends why that has made a difference in your life.
My friend Andrea, who is the first name after Andrew's and mine
on emergency contact forms for Maddy and Lucy, has a knack
for making every get-together funny and memorable. I wrote her

letter the week after my dad had been diagnosed with cancer, knowing full well I'd be drawing on Andrea and her husband, Neil, for distraction and support in the months to follow.

> You became much more than the "can you watch my kids for an hour" friends; you became the "Mom, can we go over to Andrea and Neil's to see what they're doing?" friends because our girls love you as much as we do. And why wouldn't they, with the shared adventures: family trips to the mountains for winter fun, sure, but all the little adventures, to the burger joint and to Ikea and walks around the block with sparklers and skateboards on New Year's Eve. My family is completely conditioned now to expect hilarity whenever we all get together. That's pretty cool—especially at a time like this. I'll be taking advantage of the built-in laughter insurance when I get back from Rochester, whenever that is.

My friend Laurie does needlepoint for fun and meditation, so when she came upon the perfect pattern for her friend Lisa ("All you need is love and a good cup of coffee"), she told me she decided to send the final product along with a thank-you letter for all that Lisa has brought into her life.

Laurie says that in her letter she "thanked Lisa for being a daily source of kindness, friendship, and generosity, in both material and spiritual ways. She is a fellow sober person, and I thanked her for showing me how to share the best parts of this life with others, because that is what she shares with me." Laurie adds, "Lisa makes receiving help, support, and friendship from her as easy a process as it can be, which is not ever going to be 100 percent comfortable for me. I am learning to receive gracefully in this phase of my life, and she has helped me smooth off some of those rough edges I developed over years of living on the defensive. Not only does this make me a better partner in all areas of life—professionally, and in love, family, and friends—but it helps me pass this gift along to others." All those thoughts went into the letter that Laurie wrote and sent.

Laurie found that the exercise of writing out her appreciation for a friend with whom she is in digital or phone contact almost every day was more powerful than she expected. "Sitting down to write a letter out to Lisa gave me time to clarify what I really wanted to say, which is not always the case when I'm shooting off my mouth, no matter how well-intentioned I am," says Laurie. "I had to transmit it to paper, and only worry a tiny bit about my messy handwriting, and whether I'd used the correct pen, which is a basic worry over the decades of my life. It felt very pre-2000s, in the best way, and I wondered to myself, 'Why did I stop doing this?' Oh right, the internet."

Laurie's experience mirrored my own. There are things we can express in writing that we simply do not communicate the same way in spoken words or in bits and bytes of digital communication.

While many of these close friendships for which I was grateful had roots in our kids' schoolyard, there are lots of places you may have met your people. The company break room, the Weight Watchers meeting, at the neighborhood barbecue . . . and the internet. Funny to think that if I'd undertaken this project ten years earlier I might never have sent my batch of Tiny Texter thank-you notes.

The Tiny Texters are a group of humor writers scattered all over the country, whose blogs I started reading voraciously eight or nine years ago. When I found one of their posts particularly funny or moving, I'd leave a comment, and they began to do the same on my blog. I started to feel like I knew these ladies a little bit, even if we'd never met in person and they lived in Maryland or Minneapolis. In 2011, I worked up the nerve to attend my first blogging conference, in San Diego, in part because some of these writers would be there. One of these women sat down at a long table near the hotel pool and tweeted her location, a few more rotated in, and for the next 72 hours, that long table became the place where all those blog posts and comments morphed into three-dimensional, living friendships for me.

The Tiny Texters—we've now moved the conversations into a group text that has sustained for years—are the people to whom I turn when I can't figure out where to submit an essay, or need someone to brainstorm a title with me, or wonder whether it should be spelled "Listener's" or "Listeners'." We also exchange dinner recipes, check in on the health of each other's parents and the schoolyard situations of each other's kids, and vote on which pair of shoes to buy based on texted pictures of the two choices that just made our phones light up. And although much of our friendship takes place on our phones, the friends to whom I wrote in this group have had real impact IRL. That's as good a test as any of which of your online people may deserve a thank-you letter.

Ann pulled my name out of a hat at an open mic night she hosted and ignited my love of live readings. Wendi is a serious student of comedy and induced me to treat humor writing with respect, deliberation, and ambition. Liz and I room together at an annual writing conference and buck each other up on the days it feels like everyone around us has become their own media empire while we're still farting around in the margins.

There are many things to hate about the internet, and I'm not just talking about googling "rash cream" once and having a related ad follow you for the rest of your days. (It was an allergic reaction, OK, Google? Unlike your ads, it went away.) But the ability to connect with people across the state, the country, and the world who share your passions and interests, people whom you find via Twitter, a Facebook group, or an email listserv, is pretty magical. I'm always amused when a friend mentions someone she follows religiously on social media who, like her, is big into flowers, or fashion, or fonts, like I should know who exactly that is. For good and for bad, we can all find our tribes online. Mailing actual physical letters to people with whom so much of your interaction takes place digitally can be particularly special.

By the time you get to the end of your letters to your closest friends, your childhood friends, and your hang-in-there friends, you should have a gratifying reminder of the kaleidoscopic colors of the network of people in your life who have sustained you.

Ready to make those colors really pop?

Past Friends

If you have managed to keep every single friend you've ever made, you can skip this section and go to brunch. Make a reservation for you and your 849,452 chums.

But if you, like me, have lost a few along the way, this is the part of the project where you can take a moment to reflect on what you've learned about yourself from those losses. Since you are under no obligation to mail all your thank-you letters, you can afford to be expansive. Who were the friends who taught you something important but are no longer in your life to see the ramifications of those lessons?

In romantic relationships, there's a built-in expectation that the end of the road may come. In friendships? Almost always a surprise.

Are there friends who betrayed you and taught you something about the importance of trust? Who made questionable lifestyle choices that helped clarify what was healthy for you? Who stole a girlfriend or boyfriend away? We've all had moments of disappointment in our friendships (except for you there at your big brunch. Drink your Bloody Mary and zip it). Learning a good lesson from those moments is your consolation prize. Writing a thank-you letter about it morphs it into a story you control and to which you can return.

In college, I had a friend who was funny, whip-smart, and beautiful. She had many good qualities but possessed a maddening sense of entitlement that demanded much and offered little in return. It took me years to figure out how one-sided our friendship was, because she was so damn interesting that it kept distracting me from the inequity at the heart of the friendship. When I finally awoke to the problem and confronted her in a fiery public blowup when we were in our early twenties, the residue of that fight held a beautiful truth: *I don't have enough time to spend with the people who actually like me. Why would I waste one second of it on people who don't?* That's been a mantra for me ever since.

I'll draw a distinction here between former friends—the ones with whom our relationship has fizzled out absent any real animosity—and ex-friends, the ones from whom we've taken a permanent and deliberate break. Writing a thank-you letter to people in the former friend category could be a creative and effective way to breathe life into a moribund friendship that simply got neglected. And just like chocolate chips and tonic water, it's never a bad idea to have an extra stash of friends lying around.

When it comes to mailing these letters to ex-friends, though, I don't see why you would; they are not worth a Forever stamp. But without having had them in your life, how would you know the true value of the ones you've kept?

FEELINGS FOR FRIENDS

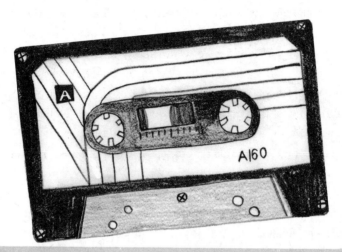

We're Going to Be Friends—
 White Stripes
Friends—Whodini
You're My Best Friend—Queen
Count on My Love—Liz Phair
The Promise—When in Rome
With a Little Help from My
 Friends—The Beatles
You've Got a Friend—Carole King
I'll Be There—Jackson 5

Friends in Low Places—Garth Brooks
California Friends—The Regrettes
Thank You Friends—Big Star
Best Friend—SOFI TUKKER feat.
 NERVO, The Knocks & Alisa Ueno
That's What Friends Are For—
 Dionne Warwick
Thank You for Being a Friend—
 Andrew Gold
For Good—Wicked soundtrack

CHAPTER 4

LESSONS FROM LOVES

If you have lived, take thankfully the past.

—JOHN DRYDEN

In the last week before Maddy left for freshman year of college, I was driving with her on an errand near our home when I had the thought that must occur to all parents just before a child moves out for the first time.

Have I missed anything?

Andrew and I spent eighteen years of parenting cramming every lesson we could into her, everything we felt she would need to know as a fully formed adult, and we had only a few days left before she moved out.

I clutched the steering wheel as I realized in a sudden panic: I had forgotten to tell Maddy why it is nice to be in love.

So much of parenting children on the topic of romantic relationships in the modern age is fear based. Don't talk online with people you don't know! Don't exchange pictures—you never know where they will end up! Abstain, but if you indulge, practice safe sex! Keep an eye on your friends if you go to a party together and leave no girl/boy behind when it's time to go! Get an HPV vaccine! Don't ever accept a drink from a stranger at a party, and if you must drink, the only safe choice is a beer that you open yourself and cover with your thumb at all times in case someone tries to slip a roofie into it! Make Proud Choices!*

Hello, Terror, thanks for coming along to chaperone my date.

That day in the car, it occurred to me that I had never once talked to either child about the deliciousness of being someone's something special. I had never talked with them about the confidence and excitement that falling in love can suddenly bring into your life, like the moment when the *Wizard of Oz* goes from black-and-white to color. That a mutually satisfying sex life with someone with whom you are in a loving, committed relationship is a treasure beyond value. I had never told them that if you choose carefully, you can let go of the pain of a broken heart and look back at your exes with a sense of gratitude for what they brought into your life when they were still a part of it.

So, I started talking. It is a testament to Maddy's good nature that when she emerged from the car at Target twenty minutes later, she did not run to the store's security guard and ask to be protected from the crazy blonde behind the wheel of the station wagon who still had at least four additional points to make in her spontaneous TED Talk.

* All things that Maddy and Lucy will 100 percent attest that I have said to them, multiple times. "Make Proud Choices" was the actual curriculum name of one of their middle school sex-ed programs, so we just use that as our family catch-all phrase.

And when I got home that afternoon, I added a few more names to my list of thank-you letters to write that fall.

A note: I did not send any of these letters. In some cases, I would not have known where to send them. (I know, right? Facebook is falling down on the job.) But even when I did, my goal in writing these letters was not to open up a big, wriggly can of worms. It was to recognize formative relationships in my life, express my gratitude for them, and move on. Or, as I wrote to one of the guys:

> I don't plan to mail this to you, because it would be too weird, but maybe by writing this I'll put some good vibes in the universe that will translate to your getting an excellent parking space right in front of your office today.

The categories I'm suggesting in this chapter aren't necessarily mutually exclusive—it's not like you are collecting fifty state quarters and are incomplete without Rhode Island. Think of them more as noteworthy facets of the messy, frustrating, glorious human personalities that you've encountered along the road thus far. And, of course, if you married the first person with whom you ever held hands, you may have covered all this ground in the letter you wrote to your current partner, and you can move on to the next chapter.

But for the rest of us, the road to true love was probably paved with a couple of speed bumps, diversions, and maybe even a gravel spin-out. Hopefully, that fateful journey left you better equipped to recognize true love when you found it, or on that day when you find it in the future.

If so, that's something to be grateful for. If not, may you have at least had some character-shaping adventures that left you with enough stories to liven up a dinner party.

This section should help you cover every one of the bases. Heh-heh-heh.

The First Crush

Oh, the first. That moment when your brain, your heart, and your hips all said in unison, "WHAT IS HAPPENING?"

Of course, like most straight women of my generation, there was a permanent change to my molecular substructure the first time I saw Duran Duran's *Hungry Like the Wolf* video (JT4Evah). But, if I'm honest, the first person about whom I felt "stirrings" was Jackie Earle Haley in *Bad News Bears*.

Ten-year-old me walked into the movie theater in 1976 a jaded Little Leaguer, figuring I'd get a laugh or two out of the messier guy from *The Odd Couple*. Two hours later, I left the theater not a girl, not yet a woman, the air-hockey scene between Haley and Tatum O'Neal imprinted in my mind and, confusingly, somewhere below the waistband of my stretch plaid bellbottoms. Frankly, it wasn't until I saw Haley playing the tortured pedophile in the 2006 movie *Little Children* that I could move on.

Maybe those first crushes had an impact beyond giving your nascent love life a jump start. I was at a conference last year where novelist Katherine Center read us the most charming piece of Duran Duran fan fiction she wrote at age twelve (see Molecular Substructure, above). It involved a tour-bus breakdown in front of her house and a plucky twelve-year-old girl who not only helped them fix their bus but also prepared a delicious snack selection. The Fab Five were, of course, in her debt. Center told the audience she wrote DDFanFic because "there was someone out there who needed to read Duran Duran fan fiction: me. And it didn't exist, so I had to write it for myself." It taught her an invaluable lesson at a young age about believing in the power of stories, something this best-selling writer of six bittersweet comic novels has come to know quite well.

Remembering your first crushes can be a sweet and funny meditation on the beautiful ways our bodies and minds conspire to make us ready for the real thing. Was the object of your earliest affections the boy or girl next door? One of the members of the Bangles or the Beatles? Was it Jackie Earle Haley? I feel that.

Thanks, first crush, for kicking the machine into motion. It may not have worked out, but hey, someone had to show us where the on/off switch was.

The One Who Taught You About Good Sex

Every year at Thanksgiving, the *San Francisco Chronicle* re-runs an old column by writer Jon Carroll entitled "A Song of Thanks; A Grat Etude." It's not your run-of-the-mill Thanksgiving prayer; Carroll casts the net wide, suggesting we take a moment to be thankful for things like artists and philosophers and the time the turkey fell on the floor.

I love this column. Every November, I cut it out of the newspaper and attach it with a "Jesus Is Coming, Look Busy" magnet to my refrigerator. And when I do, I invariably take a moment in silent thanks for another person Carroll suggested in his meditation: "We all learned about good sex from somebody, and that person deserves a moment." Carroll gets credit for the fact that I remembered to include this person in my list of fifty influences in my life.

In fact, this was perhaps the most important topic I covered in my car monologue with Maddy on our way to Target, one especially critical for a young woman to hear at a time when media imagery and online channels distort expectations of what is "normal," of what "all the girls" do, and when the public discourse sends a disheartening message about the power dynamics of sexual relationships. I wanted her to understand that the sex you get to have in a relationship characterized by trust, open communication, and real, mutual affection is on an entirely different plane than the other kind, regardless of how it's portrayed in the movies and on Netflix. That each of us has every right to expect good sex and move on when it isn't present.

I know that because someone came along in my own life and taught me that lesson.

I had relationships in college with people who I knew, even then, weren't all that crazy about me. But I still equated sex with love back then, and who doesn't want to be loved? So, occasionally, even if it was bound to be disappointing, I just went with it. I knew I should probably have higher standards, but what if high standards meant I would be alone in my dorm room listening to *How Soon Is Now* by The Smiths on repeat every Saturday night? It was a conundrum, and, with a few beers in me, it was one I didn't have to solve.

And then in my early twenties, mercifully, I met someone who liked me and who eventually fell in love with me. We were friends for months before we were lovers, and from the very first time we were together, I thought, *Oh! I get it now!* He drew a bright line of demarcation between good and bad sex for me, for the rest of my life. Why you gonna eat generic chocolate in a world where Toblerone exists?

Is there someone in your past who helped you see yourself as desirable and worthy of respect? A guy or gal whose tender adoration of your body made it hum at a higher vibration? Someone who helped you understand your own worth in a way that prevented you from ever lowering your standards again—or at least, when that happened, meant you did so with your eyes open?

If this gratitude for good sex ends up being a paragraph in a letter you write to your current partner, guess what? Your sex life may get even better now. In a 2008 study on the neural basis of human social values, researchers found that gratitude correlated with higher levels of dopamine, the neurotransmitter known as the "reward" drug, in that it boosts sensations of pleasure. Dopamine also plays a role in initiating behavior. As science journalist Bethany Brookshire wrote in a 2013 article for *Slate*, "[Dopamine is] what we call salience. Salience is more than attention: It's a sign of something that needs to be paid attention *to*, something that stands out."

By expressing your gratitude for something that brings you pleasure, to a person who is the bringer of that feeling, you give them a rush of dopamine that tells them, "Do it again! Do it again!" Bow chicka wow wow.

The Meaningful Exes

Let me officially absolve you of the burden of writing a letter to every past boyfriend or girlfriend who ever gazed into your eyes. You probably have better things to do, like wash your hair or check the cupboards for leftover fun-size Halloween candy.

However, there may have been a person or two in your past who—back to those questions from Chapter 1—helped, shaped, or inspired you in some way, beyond just making out with you and letting you borrow sweatshirts. The ones who were meaningful to your development, taught you something practical, stood by you at a time when you needed help. These are the kind of people I would clump under the term "meaningful" and start writing.

One of the letters I wrote is to the boyfriend with whom I experienced the fall of the Berlin Wall in 1990. My German ex and I have always maintained a cordial friendship, and I think it is in part because we went through this formative time together. My move to Munich took place in the waning days of the Cold War, and I experienced firsthand the stuttering, dramatic, exhilarating reunion of East and West Germany. My then boyfriend lived in Berlin, and I used to fly up to see him in the city at the heart of the national transformation. We took a hammer to the Berlin Wall to help knock it down; we walked together through the Brandenburg Gate in the wee hours of New Year's Day 1990, when the East German guards unexpectedly abandoned their posts; we drove in his car through the East German countryside a few months later and gawped at the cobblestone roads and grimy Stalinist architecture that presented such a sharp contrast to cutting-edge West Berlin. On my very last night living in Germany, we saw Pink Floyd perform *The Wall* at the Wall.

I will never, ever cease to marvel that I got a front-row seat for that bit of global history. More than that, I had the privilege of seeing the once-unimaginable reunification of his country through the eyes of my West German–born boyfriend. That had to be memorialized in the unsent letter I wrote him.

Maybe you had similar bucket-list adventures with an ex. But maybe there were smaller and more personal triumphs. Did your ex take you to your first NASCAR race and unlock your need for speed? Did she share her mom's secret recipe for lemon cake, the one you bake whenever you feel low? Even if we hadn't been partners during such a historic era, my German friend was invaluable in helping his foreign-born girlfriend negotiate the formidable administrative labyrinth that is everyday life in Germany. I wrote to him:

Our relationship took place against a background of my living and working in a country where I basically knew no one, and you were such a good friend to me from that standpoint. I doubt very much whether I would have stayed in Germany for two years had I not had your counsel and advice about practical things, from paying my taxes to paying bills at the post office (What? That still seems like a super weird system to me) to obtaining residency permits and work permits.

I hope that there have been loves in your life who brought more intangible gifts to it: their confidence in you when your own faltered, a knack for timing when it came to compliments about your appearance, a discerning mind that helped you sort out some garbage from your childhood. I wrote to one ex:

> You were kind to me, you looked out for me, and you really cared about what happened to me in a way that I was unaccustomed to. If I look back at the moment in my life when I began to appreciate my own gifts and talents, and to be proud of the person I was, I think it was when you treated me with such respect and pride.

My friend Lisa is now in her fifties, happily married, a busy PTA volunteer, and raising a son, but she passed through some crazy terrain on her way to this particular point of domestic bliss. ("I ran amuck in early-eighties Hollywood" is how she summarizes it.) A few years ago, she decided to systematically reach out to her exes to take ownership and control of her own story and to find the good in these past relationships.

Lisa wrote to one ex with the intention of thanking him for putting up with so much of what she describes as the "extreme behavior" of her youth, and for coming to her aid, both financially and as a friend. The guy was surprised to receive Lisa's letter, and even more surprised that she felt apologetic. He got in touch and, Lisa says, "the situation turned quickly to him thanking me. He sees me as the catalyst for his music career and as a linchpin who shaped his life. I had no idea." Lisa added, "I literally considered myself a force of darkness and selfishness during that period, and he showed me I was wrong. It has made a continuing impact on how I see myself, and I have now been able to forgive myself for some bad choices."

One of the letters I wrote in this category was to a guy whom I was once crazy for but who, it must be said, just wasn't that into me. Not that I gave up without a rather degrading amount of effort. As I thought over the rejection that was so painful at the time, I knew this guy had been an important stepping-stone in my journey to find Andrew.

> I suspect that my short and turbulent time with you was what gave me the courage to hold out until I found someone else who checked all the boxes: smart, funny, and kind. So thank you for setting a higher standard.

As I said that day to Maddy in my Car Lecture™, "Hopefully you will choose the people you fall for because of their good qualities. Those good qualities don't go away after you break up with them." Giving credit where it is due regarding how those good qualities made your life better when you were together, and maybe even after you weren't anymore, is what this batch of letters is all about.

The Fantasy Islands

Admit it: you have stared into the middle distance while washing the dishes as a child stood nearby practicing for her third-grade recorder concert and thought, *If I were married to Scarlett Johansson, this combined housework and auditory assault would not be happening right now.* You have listened to a budget presentation at work while internally debating the merits of

Harrison Ford's 1977 Han Solo versus Alden Ehrenreich's 2018 version. And raise your hand if you have ever thought to yourself with real conviction, *Idris Elba, I would be so good for you.*

Minds wander. It is one of their favorite tricks. And sometimes the most restful, restorative places they can go is to someone with whom you have zero chance, to luxuriate in a 100 percent impossible "what if." I have a friend who calls these moments "the little happy places" of our brains, flimsy and impermanent platforms that give us a place to catch our breath as we speed down the rushing rivers of our daily lives. But platforms just the same.

I am not talking about disloyalty to your current partner. What I'm suggesting is that an active fantasy life may have been a marvelous, free coping mechanism you have employed in the past. And the people whom you meet there may deserve an (unsent) letter.

Once, when our girls attended a Montessori preschool, we got a notice that the rambling old Victorian house in Oakland where it was located needed an upgrade to its fire-alarm system. I walked up the front steps a few days later, holding hands with Maddy and Lucy, to see two of the female Montessori teachers wide-eyed and gazing upward.

There, on a ladder and focusing hard on a smoke alarm in the ceiling, was the most exquisite Fire Alarm Repair Man that God ever saw fit to create. Lithe, with mocha skin and long, shiny black hair tied neatly back into a ponytail, he rendered everyone in his immediate vicinity mute except the kids. Was that a 500-watt bulb or merely his aura blinding us? Hard to tell. Let's keep staring at him surreptitiously to see if we can figure it out. That he was polite and friendly to everyone at the school, and generally sat on a ladder three feet above us like a Greek statue on a pedestal, made it extra challenging. Do preschool first aid kits include smelling salts? They should.

For the week this company was on site fixing the smoke alarms, none of the moms could stop giggling, and the teachers were even worse. Yes, we were all relieved that the children and teachers would be safer after the van pulled away on the last day, but it was relief tinged with a real sense of loss. Au revoir, Fire Alarm Repair Man; we barely knew ye.

No one in our family has attended a Montessori school in thirteen years. But I still do a double take every time I see a white panel van with "Fire Alarms" written on the side.

Of course, this goes both ways. It is an open secret in our family that Andrew is a member of a Facebook group for young Scandinavians, although he is neither. "I somehow got added," he told me, to which I explained that when you press the "Join" button, membership will almost certainly be the outcome. He occasionally tells me that he and the young Scandinavians are meeting to fix up a cabin in Lake Tahoe, or to cure gravlax, or for a Midsommar party, and I tell him to have fun. I know he is only meeting up with Birgitta, Sigrid, and Malin in his mind, and is still available to pick Lucy up from ballet later.

Look, life can be so difficult sometimes, like pushing a bag of boulders uphill in a hurricane. It takes a toll. So, whatever gets you through, and does not hurt you or anyone else, is fair game as a coping strategy. These days, my mom keeps a 5" x 7" photo in her purse at all times, not of my father, but of the aforementioned John Denver impersonator, standing with his arm around her after a recent performance. Mom gets frustrated that a lot of actual memories of her actual husband have skittered away from her, but gazing at Fake John Denver always puts a smile on her face. And I'm all for it.

When you think back over your life, who were the people you visited momentarily in your "little happy places" to gird your loins for the next day? What were the chasms they helped you cross when you needed a distraction? These people may only exist for you on a movie screen or in a novel or sitting three rows ahead on your bus ride into work, but they've given you the gift of mental escape when you needed it. Go ahead and give thanks.

The Good Riddances

Here we are: the people in our lives who really earned that "ex." As with the Past Friends category, your life may have been shaped and inspired by people who taught you what to avoid. It is like the human version of phototropism, the phenomenon that causes plants to grow toward the light and away from the darkness.

This section isn't about the loves that just faded away. These are the people who taught you that you deserve someone who can hold a job, shower regularly, and treat your mom with respect. Their (hopefully short-lived) poor treatment acted as a whetstone for your ability to weed out the losers and dump the users. It wasn't fun while it lasted, actually. But you didn't make that mistake a second time. Or a third time, anyway.

If you choose to write the people who fall into this category for you, it may take a hard lean into that idea of forgiveness first, so you can clear enough space for gratitude. No one says that will be easy.

But writing down the lessons that you learned from your Good Riddances and reflecting on how those have carried you to where you are today is a chance to reframe and reclaim these relationships as victories, not (just) time and energy wasted.

LESSONS FROM LOVES

Crush On You—The Jets
I'm Not a Girl, Not Yet
  a Woman—Britney Spears
The Night We Met—Lord Huron
Somebody to Love—Queen
In Your Eyes—Peter Gabriel
When You Were Mine—Night
  Terrors of 1927
You Wear It Well—Rod Stewart
Penelope Cruz—Bob Schneider

The Roughest Toughest Game in
  the World—Split Enz
A Letter to Elise—The Cure
Love Ain't for Keeping—The Who
Every Time I Hear That Song—
  Brandi Carlile
I Can't Make You Love Me/Nick
  of Time—Bon Iver
thank u, next—Ariana Grande
Unsent—Alanis Morrissette

CHAPTER 5

INSPIRATIONS FROM INFLUENCERS

Each of us has cause to think with great gratitude
of those who have lighted the flame within us.
—ALBERT SCHWEITZER

If you were to ask a random person on the street for whom in their life they were thankful, I bet 90 percent of them would say something along the lines of, "Family and friends." They are the big, obvious categories, the ones that take up most of our mindshare, a perfectly appropriate answer to the question. That's why we started this project with those people.

But what about the dentist who spotted and fixed a problem with your teeth before it turned into a major, weeks-off-from-work medical issue for you? Or the teacher who helped you transfer out of her French class and into a science class down the hallway when she saw which way le wind was blowing on your grades? Or the boss who placed you into a job you ended up loving, more confident than you were of your capabilities?

For me, this was the part of the thank-you-letter writing project that felt like it rewired my brain the most, because it got me into the habit of looking for the myriad, unseen ways we are supported by people who have no expectation of an expression of gratitude. Helping us is the job that pays their bills, in some cases. You could argue that you do not owe these people anything beyond the opportunity to practice their profession on you.

I would argue back that the people in this part of your list probably suffer the biggest gap between deserving thank-you letters and ever once receiving them. If you consider for fifteen seconds what your life would truly look like sans the more memorable teachers, medical professionals, and role models you've encountered on your path, you'll get a very quick measure of the thanks you owe them.

Besides, this far into the process of writing your letters, or at least thinking about doing so, you will have noticed that your stores of gratitude are not depleted. The more you give it away, the more it seems to fill back up. And science shows that where gratitude is given, happiness tends to linger longer.

In a 2005 study published in *American Psychologist,* researchers tested the durability of feelings of happiness after subjects wrote a gratitude letter and then performed a onetime, in-person "gratitude visit" to deliver it. They contrasted this practice with having participants record in a journal three things that went well for them each day, for a one-week period.

The participants who wrote and hand-delivered the gratitude letter experienced a 10 percent jolt of increased happiness right afterward, but that increase was halved within a week, and six months later there was no discernible increase at all.

In contrast, the people who did the ongoing, daily practice of identifying their "three good things" didn't have as high a bump in immediate happiness as the gratitude-visit people did—they were only 2 percent happier than before, after one week.

But in follow-up tests, this group's happiness levels kept on increasing, from being 5 percent happier at one month to 9 percent happier at six months. And this was even though their instructions were to journal their three good things for only seven days and then stop. Here was my favorite part of this study: participants enjoyed the daily writing exercise so much that they just kept on doing it on their own. "Alert in Lab 6! We have some rogue Gratefuls on the loose! Condition Yellow!"

I'm no scientist, but I think if we combine the letter-writing practice of the first group with the ongoing nature of the second group's gratitude journal we will have engaged the Flux Capacitor on our happiness levels. If my calculations are correct.

The point is, you can afford to be magnanimous in adding another name to your list. Who are the unnoticed heroes and helpers in your life? Here's a hint: they are everywhere you look on a random day.

In School

I am what you call a late bloomer, in literary terms. I always loved reading and writing, but I spent a largely satisfying seventeen years working in marketing and product management before deciding at around forty that what I *really* wanted was to be a writer. It meant starting from scratch.

Except it didn't, because my high school AP English teacher was a lady named Mrs. Green.

The many writing workshops, classes, and conferences I have attended, the books on the craft of writing I've devoured, and the millions of words I've written in the past dozen years to improve my skills all sit atop the solid foundation of writing and literary analysis Mrs. Green taught me in the 1983–1984 school year. We dissected, memorized, and performed passages from *Macbeth*, we broke the spines on our Strunk & Whites, and every time we handed in the first draft of a paper, her response was, "Good start. Now shorten it by a third." Anyone in class with me that year will remember the time Mrs. Green gave one of her exuberant literary lectures and mistakenly yelled the word "orgasm" when she meant to say "organism," which was far too much for a roomful of seventeen-year-olds to handle with any kind of chill. We loved coming to class to see what would happen next.

Mrs. Green is the reason that throughout my business career, my favorite assignments were the few that involved writing. I once turned in an annual strategic marketing plan for our software product that had narrative structure, foreshadowing, and a thrilling denouement. A senior manager in another division who had read it stopped by my office to tell me it was the best thing he had read all year, which I recognized was more of an indictment of his reading habits than a compliment about my writing, but still.

Mrs. Green made me a writer during the Reagan era; it just took me until the George W. Bush era to figure it out.

Teachers have probably never been given the credit they

are due for their devotion and time in the face of unimaginable challenges. In the current age of educational budget shortfalls and onerous testing requirements, the gap between the thanks a special teacher is owed and what they receive seems particularly galling. Do you really think a shiny red apple for Mr. Cortez the physics teacher is enough, when he is spending his own money on graph paper for the classroom and working at Starbucks to make ends meet? That's why letters to the amazing teachers you—and your children—have encountered over the years are a wonderful place to start for this section.

Who were those educators who saw something special in you, who made you excited to come to class, who held you to such high academic standards that they inadvertently made everything else that came after seem easy?

When she wrote her own batch of milestone thank-you letters, my friend Melisa included on her list both a memorable fifth-grade teacher, and a high school German teacher who had passed away a few years earlier. Melisa says, "Everyone agrees that teaching is one of the most noble professions, but this was a way to take a small action to let some important teachers in my life know how much they impacted me and made me who I am today, even if the letters didn't end up in their hands." Melisa plans to send the letter for her late German teacher to the woman's daughter. "I think her daughter would probably like to read how much of an impact her mom made on me over the four years she was my teacher."

Of course, it isn't just the teachers in school who make a difference in our lives. There are coaches and counselors, lunch ladies and librarians. My high school had an incredibly popular security guard who, I imagine, might be the first person some classmates think about when they remember their glory days at Brighton High School. The educational system through which you passed surely influenced the person you have become.

And schools are not the only buildings in which we come across instructors who change us. Do your piano teacher, your drill instructor, and/or your karate sensei belong on your list?

A thank-you letter to the individuals who helped you uncover your talents and buff them to a high shine would be a fitting way to let them know you were paying attention in their master class.

In the Doctor's Office

As much as people seem to dread the downsides of middle age, I've found one aspect to really embrace: deliberate and active appreciation for my health. Because every few months something else breaks or falls off.

First, it was the plantar fasciitis, then the frozen shoulder, then a fun bout with chronic dry eye that made me look for six months like I was stoned, all day long. I am like a slow-moving glacier, powerless to do anything but plow through whatever aging-related ailment is next in my path.

During the year I wrote my letters, whenever I found myself in a doctor's waiting room with nothing but *US Weekly* magazines from a decade earlier to distract me (no, 2006, it turns out Angie and Brad did *not* have what it takes to last forever) I had cause to think about the medical professionals in my life who have done the necessary, unacknowledged work of keeping my family and me upright and functioning. C'mon. These are people who handle your pee, poke your bunions, and check your prostate, and you're not even going to give them a tip of the hat?

Who are the medical professionals who have eased your pains, cured your ailments, and shepherded your health decisions over the years? Was there someone who got you onto the right medication just in time, or helped you finally break a bad habit, or called you after hours just to check in?

Maybe these special doctors and nurses haven't cared for you, but rather for your aging parents or children; consider how your own life would be different had they not been so skilled in caring for your loved ones. Remember that 100-letters-in-100-days gratitude project that Shannon did? It all started with the simple act of writing the doctor who had cared for her late mom with such compassion. "I went to the Denver Botanical Gardens with the intention of buying a memorial brick for my mom, because she was a gardener," explains Shannon. "And someone said to me, 'By the way, did you know she already has one here?'" Shannon found the brick, inscribed with her mother's name and the words, "Creative, Intelligent, and Kind." Her mother's physician had quietly dedicated it after Shannon's mom passed away. Shannon says, "I just spent a few moments thinking about this doctor and his experience, and I decided I needed to write him." That first pebble eventually rippled outward in the form of ninety-nine more letters.

I wrote a thank-you letter to the obstetrician who safely delivered Maddy and Lucy into the world. That is a ridiculously small sentence to describe the two most staggering blessings of my life: healthy babies. And while I had mostly uncomplicated deliveries, the risks during even straightforward births like mine are real. No one should take for granted that they will end successfully. I wrote to my OB, in part:

> Both times I was scared, tired, and in pain, and both times you exhibited so much confidence and matter-of-fact calm that I was made braver, stronger, and more determined to get through it. I do remember the pain, but it is a pinprick compared to the feeling of pride and rush of emotion in finally meeting those baby girls—just like my mom used to tell me, when I was a skeptical teenager who swore I would never ever ever never in a million years have kids.
>
> Thank you, thank you, thank you for delivering my two girls safely. I will always be in your debt for that.

What was remarkable about sending this letter was the one I received in return. My OB, Dr. Laurie Green, has been delivering babies in San Francisco for thirty-five years and runs a foundation that connects retired doctors with clinics in underserved communities. I once read an interview with her where she estimated that she's delivered 17,000 babies and said that her last vacation was in 2000. Dr. Green is someone who should be getting absolutely hammered with "Thank You!" bouquets from 1-800-Flowers, is my point. But she still took the time to write back to me after receiving my letter, which tells me that she does not receive them nearly as often as she should.

> Thank you so much for your beautiful note—which I opened and read today as Women's Marches took place across

the country. I'm honored to be among the 50 people you mention. It has been hard work and practice but what a joy to hear one makes a difference!

According to a 2018 survey from Medscape, 42 percent of physicians reported feeling burnout from the demands of their work, and 15 percent experienced some form of depression. But a patient's gratitude can mitigate some of that. A 2017 study of the impact that patients' appreciation can have on burnout in nurses showed that expressions of gratitude and support from patients is highly beneficial, especially for nurses who work in high-stress environments like emergency departments.

A few weeks after Lucy had recovered completely from her weeklong stint in the hospital for a respiratory virus as an infant (during which my friend Jill performed that emergency *Vogue* and latte delivery), I strapped Lu into the front pack, and we went out to buy a sheet cake for the nurse's station at Children's Hospital in Oakland. We headed to the floor where doctors and nurses had tended our tiny girl through an illness that I mercifully learned only after the fact could be fatal.

The nurses on the ward were gobsmacked as they looked at the big vanilla cake that read, "Thank You Doctors and Nurses."

"No one ever does this," said one of the women who had monitored our daughter's oxygen levels, administered the life-saving antibiotics she needed, and stayed in the room with our baby so I could run across the street every morning for a coffee and a deep, centering breath of fresh air before the next 23.75-hour bedside vigil. "No one."

We live in an age of science miracles, when diseases that

would have carried off our foremothers and forefathers in a week are preventable with a vaccine or treatable with a pill. Doctors and nurses (and home health-care aides and physical therapists and acupuncturists and reiki specialists and whoever else is a teammate in the effort to keep you healthy and whole) are the ones who connect us to those cures. The professionals who do it with wisdom, compassion, and simple human understanding stand out, and they deserve to know it.

In the Workplace

One of my earliest jobs was working at a restaurant in Rochester housed in a historic building next to the Erie Canal. I was on a team of high school typists who spent after-school hours typing addresses out of the Rochester telephone book onto envelopes, into which we then stuffed marketing flyers.

It wasn't the monotonous nature of the work that got to me, or the imperious supervisor who inspected our envelopes with the warmth of a Gestapo agent. It was that the typists worked on a little wooden platform enclosed with chicken wire. Yes, I was caged. Some afternoons, after our humorless boss left for the day, the restaurant's bakers took pity on us and passed tiny corn muffins through the holes in the chicken wire. Strangely enough, the corn muffin feedings didn't really make us teenage typists feel better about the situation.

Anyone with a similarly lousy job story knows how much a great boss and cage-free employment is worth. What you may not realize is how infrequently any of us remember to express gratitude for it.

In the 2012 gratitude survey from the John Templeton Foundation, only 10 percent of respondents expressed thanks or gratitude to their coworkers on a daily basis, and only 7 percent did so to their bosses. While almost nine out of ten respondents said that expressing gratitude to colleagues made them feel happier and more fulfilled, 60 percent of respondents never expressed gratitude in the workplace at all.

This is what we call an opportunity, people. Look to your left and right, and then check behind the door in the break room. You may find some coworkers, employees, and bosses to add to your list. After all: if you work full-time, you likely spend more time each day with your work colleagues than with your family members.

These workplace thank-you letters can go in any direction: if you are the boss, consider the impact it would have to express your gratitude to the employees who keep things humming. One of the most moving thank-you letters I've read was written by Charles Jack Price. He was the administrator of Parkland Memorial Hospital in Dallas, Texas, on November 27, 1963, when Governor John Connally, President John Kennedy, and alleged assailant Lee Harvey Oswald were all rushed there for treatment. Afterward, Price sent a memo to all employees at Parkland Memorial that summarized the significance of what the prior two days meant for the charity hospital. Among other things, it had become the temporary seat of the US government, the temporary site of the government of the State of Texas, and the site of both the death of the thirty-fifth president and the ascendancy of the thirty-sixth president. Perhaps most impressive, the hospital continued to serve all its other patients. Price went on to write to his team:

Our pride is not that we were swept up by the whirlwind of tragic history, but that when we were, we were not found wanting.

At a time when Parkland employees were surely traumatized, Price's deliberate recognition of their professionalism and good work must have gone a long way toward helping them recover and continue to do their jobs with pride.

It doesn't have to be an enormous achievement to merit recognition. Unbeknownst to me until I started writing this book, my brother, Larry, has been handwriting thank-you notes to his employees for years. He heads up the facilities division for a large Rochester corporation with locations around the country and travels frequently to its various sites.

Larry says, "The work of planning flights and hotels and then doing the receipts afterward is a terrific pain to me. On my trips I often send a note to our travel team and to the admin I work with. Knowing that those things get handled correctly just about 100 percent of the time is a huge stress relief for me, and the time to write the note pales in comparison to the planning and administrative work for the trip." Oftentimes he throws a $1 or $2 lottery scratch-off ticket into the envelope, which he then drops into interoffice mail. Aside from the obvious risk of one of his employee's hitting it big on the lottery and quitting, Larry says, "The best feeling I get is if I happen to walk by an employee's work station and I see a thank-you note I wrote pinned up in their space."

And never underestimate what it means to a great boss to hear the words "thank you."

I once had the opportunity to profile Wall Street pioneer Margo Alexander. Margo landed in the macho, rough-and-tumble financial services industry in the early 1970s and, through tenacity, brains, and sheer hard work, became the first woman to head a top-ranked Wall Street research department, the first woman to run a major trading desk, and one of the first women to head a large asset management business. She retired in 2003 as chairman and CEO of UBS Global Asset Management, one of the most senior women on Wall Street.

Behind the scenes and throughout her career, Margo leveraged her stature to make the financial services industry more welcoming to women, both by influencing organizational policy and through her hiring and promotional practices. People I interviewed who worked with and for Margo all mentioned her determination to create more inclusive and diverse work environments in the male-dominated financial services industry, shouldering doors open and holding them for the people who came after her.

The quantitative aspects of Margo's career in finance, which included helming the turnaround of a struggling major asset-management business in the 1990s, would have been enough to earn her the accolades and awards with which she has rightfully been recognized. But when I asked her what accomplishments she found most meaningful in her long and exemplary career, Margo said it was her ability to engage at a personal level with her colleagues and employees. She mentioned that she still receives the occasional thank-you note out of the blue from past employees whom she has not seen in decades. "People say, 'You were the greatest boss I ever had,'" she told me. "That really means something to me."

If there was an exemplary boss in your past or present, what a wonderful act it would be to let them know exactly how they made a difference for you. In writing about the specific reasons—perhaps they accommodated your need for flexibility at a time when you were caring for an ailing relative, or they promoted you into a role that you weren't sure you were ready for (but were), or had your back when you were treated unfairly in the workplace—they get positive reinforcement for the best attributes they bring to the office party, and you get a recollection of the everyday support and help that made a difference in your life.

During the first dot-com era, I worked at one of those tech companies that made the bubble burst. We were all about "synergy" and "leverage" and tons of employee perks, and not so much about "revenue" or "sustainable business models." At a holiday party we attended six months after I had joined the company, there were stilt-walking jugglers and prime rib stations and sushi chefs and two live bands. My husband the banker looked around the festivities in open-mouthed wonder and said, "How do you guys make money, again?" I had no answer.

What I loved about that job wasn't all the crazy perks, like team-building days at Disneyland or keggers on Fridays. It was my boss, Brenda, who communicated clearly, publicly credited her team members for their ideas, and offered as much flexibility as we needed, as long as we got our jobs done. Maddy was a toddler then, and I worked part-time, and if ever I came in early for a mandatory company-wide meeting or stayed late to finish up an assignment, Brenda nagged me until I took some comp time off. She was even more accommodating once I told her I was pregnant with our second child.

The night before a huge and, in retrospect, inevitable company-wide layoff in 2000, when I was nine months pregnant with Lucy, she did me the greatest kindness of all: she called me at home to give me the news in advance, making sure first that (a) Andrew was home and (b) I was lying down to take the call. She was terribly worried about the impact the news might have on my late-stage pregnancy and, I suspect, went against all corporate guidance she had been given about keeping mum until the next day's job massacre started. When I lumbered in the following morning, I had mostly processed the shock and was able to park myself front and center at the all-hands announcement, where I could fix the CEO with my most guilt-inducing stink eye while dramatically massaging my giant belly.

I miss the prime rib parties, I miss the Disneyland trips, but Brenda, I miss you most of all. You were my first real example of how to be a kind, ethical person in a field not known for either attribute.

Your list of names in this section could even include the lousy bosses or terrible coworkers who drove you out of a job into the waiting embrace of another profession that turned out to be your true calling. *Thanks for being the burr under my saddle! Were it not for your particular brand of special, I might still be crying in my cubicle at three p.m. every day instead of running a whole department at my new job, where we get chair massages on Fridays!*

If there are workplace allies who clock you in when you are late, a subordinate who offers to spend her lunch break making that Excel chart with which you are struggling, or a mentor who encourages you to sign up for professional-development classes and arranges to have the company pay for it, why not write them a note to let them know that you don't take it for granted?

In Those Who Inspire

On back-to-school nights when the girls were in elementary school, there was inevitably one hallway wall decorated with a glittered-out sign that read "Our Heroes." Underneath hung posters where kids had drawn and written about the people who inspired them, and I loved seeing the diversity and quirkiness of who made the wall of fame. Neil Armstrong, Madam C.J. Walker, Julia Child, maybe Grandma or Grandpa. When you are a kid, you are expected and encouraged to have people you look up to for models of behavior and accomplishment; you're pretty short, after all.

As an adult, you may still have those kinds of people in your life, but it's unlikely you're drawing a picture of them and writing a one-paragraph summary about why. Until now, that is. Stop sniffing the glue sticks, keep your hands to yourself, and think about who has set a positive example for how you move through the world.

The first letter I wrote in this category was to my minister. I attend an Episcopal church that has both a bracing sense of social justice and a bracing sense of humor. One of the sayings that gets bandied about from the pulpit often is, "The church has left the building," as in, don't just sit in the pews and think good thoughts; get out there into the community and perpetrate good actions. Our church lobbies city officials for equitable transportation policies in Oakland, knits hats and socks for the homeless to whom we serve lunch at 32nd and San Pablo each month, and marches together in the Oakland Pride parade with a rainbow banner that says, "All Are Welcome."

As for the sense of humor, I will give but one example: We needed to upgrade our bathrooms to become ADA compliant so that we could be more welcoming to members with disabilities. The fundraising included a gold-painted and bedazzled commode prominently placed in the front foyer under a banner that read "Let My People Go."

Religion has been perverted and twisted to such dark purposes throughout human history; if you're not somewhat skeptical about embracing organized religion, you're probably not thinking about it with the degree of doubt that real belief invites. And while I had grown up in the Episcopal church, I never felt particularly connected to my faith. Once I moved out of my parents' home for college, I only went to church on Christmas and Easter. As for Andrew, who has even less of a religious bent than I did, we had an agreement: if he would marry me in a church, which did feel important, I would never ask him to attend it with me again. I have (mostly) kept my end of that bargain.

Then I got pregnant with Maddy and panicked about whether we were capable of raising a good human being. Church seemed like a good place to find backup, and at seven months pregnant I started attending St. John's because it was the closest Episcopal church to our house. As I wrote to Father Scott:

What I only grew to realize and appreciate over time was that I was now in the congregation of a gifted minister and someone who would inspire me to more openly and fervently embrace my faith. I grew up in the Episcopal church, but church wasn't something we talked about much; we certainly never uttered the word "Jesus" unless it came right after a toe was stubbed or a driver cut us off. As a young adult, I probably went inside a church three times a year.

And I kept St. John's at a bit of an arm's distance for a while, too, not getting involved beyond bringing Maddy to the nursery and Sunday School, and sticking around for coffee hour some days. But Sunday after Sunday, year after year, I felt this burning flame of faith burn a little brighter and higher, and so much of it was due to the tone you set at St. John's: welcoming, challenging, full of humility.

As a writer, I marvel at your skills in weaving together disparate threads, in making complex concepts accessible, and in keeping humor alive somewhere in everything you talk about. I am inspired by your energy and commitment to social good, and the way in which that translates into on-the-ground opportunities for your parishioners to be involved.

I take tremendous comfort in my faith these days. This has been a hard year, with my dad's death, and to be honest I don't pray as much as I used to. It just doesn't come naturally right now. But I show up at church as much as I can, I listen to your preaching, and I sit there in a community that I know is holding me up until I'm ready again to "pray without ceasing." And that is a gift beyond value.

Who are the people in your life to whom you look for spiritual support and guidance, or who navigate the world in a way that inspires you? Think far beyond the walls of places of worship: a motivational author, a meditation teacher, an AA sponsor.

As a writer, many of my role models are authors. Reading has been my escape, my comfort, my adventure since I was four years old and sounding out words from the flash cards Mom made for me. No author's books have provided me more sheer pleasure per word than Jane Austen, whose dog-eared works anchor their own central section of my living room bookshelf. One of my finest achievements in mothering was the day I heard preschool-aged Maddy and her friend Maya arguing about which one of them got to be Elizabeth Bennet and which one Jane in their game of "Pwide and Pijidis." (I was relieved nobody was trying to be Lydia.)

The exercise of writing to Jane Austen was wildly entertaining to this nerd, as I considered what I would need to explain to her about the differences between the times in which she lived and mine.

Hello from two hundred years after your death. Can you believe that "Jane Austen" has become a household name, not just in England but in the colony across the Atlantic Ocean that declared independence the year after you were born? Such was the genius of your writing and your understanding of the human condition and, in this much less romantic age, the power of a dashing hero.

By the standards (and life expectancies) of your day, I would be considered an ancient crone, but in the current era, thanks to modern medicine, I may yet have a few decades to conquer. So, I have taken it upon myself to reflect with thanks on the people who have brightened or altered the state of my life in a significant way, and authors belong in the ranks alongside friends and family. I assure you that, *Northanger Abbey*'s satirical views of novels to the contrary, the reading of novels is now accepted, encouraged, admired. Or was, until the invention of digital electronic devices (I will trouble you with the definition of none of those words) distracted us to a point where even reading a news article is too time-consuming.

Regardless, let me assure you: your writing has not only withstood the test of time but improved the times in which it has been experienced. In my case, your books draw me back again and again, and each time I reread them I think, "There is still nothing better in the world than a Jane Austen heroine." Flawed, funny, smart, seeking betterment in material and spiritual ways: the Elizabeth Bennets and Lady Susans and Anne Elliots in the worlds you created have always struck me as entirely sympathetic and entertaining.

You were also a feminist—someone who believes that women and men should have equal rights and opportunities—before the word had even been coined. Through the eyes of your heroines we observe the systems and strictures that kept women in their place, but it is done so deftly and lightly that we see none of the tricks yet feel all the outrage. That is an amazing feat, and that it was accomplished by a woman who was herself limited by the same systems makes it even more so.

I had read a couple of your novels in high school, but it wasn't until a college class—yes, women not only go to college now but do so at rates slightly higher than men do—called "British Women Writers of the 19th Century" that I was able to do a deep dive into your work, taught by a female professor who helped us uncover the meaning and beauty in your words. So, I was a committed fan well before the film adaptations of your work (think of "film adaptation" as a sort of theatre show) introduced us to Colin Firth as Mr. Darcy, Ciarán Hinds as Colonel Wentworth, Hugh Grant as Edward Farrars . . . let me just say to you, Miss Austen, that the women of the twentieth and twenty-first centuries thank you for creating characters that led to those particular men running around before us in ruffled blouses and breech pants.

Who are your favorite writers, musicians, athletes, activists, artists? The creative people whose work carries you beyond yourself, whose vision helps you clarify your own, whose talent and hard work have combined to create a body of work that brings you simple joy?

In this category I also included my favorite music writer and memoirist, Rob Sheffield, and the late humor columnist Erma Bombeck, whom I like to call St. Erma. (Her miracles were many and documented in the pages of newspapers everywhere.) These are writers who have not just entertained me in my life, but whose technique I've studied in the hopes of becoming better at my own craft. Both weave humor into their writing in a way that is enlightening, empathetic, and uproariously funny, not an easy trifecta to pull off.

I also wrote a letter to my favorite musician, Neil Finn of the antipodean bands Split Enz and Crowded House. I told him:

I discovered Split Enz in 1980 when I was fourteen, climbed aboard the Neil Finn Fan Bus, and have never disembarked. I've seen you play live in so many cities, in every iteration of your bands, in venues from the grungy Tower Theater in Philly in 1987 to the plush rocking-chair comfort of San Francisco's Palace of Fine Arts in 2014. Your musicality, your songwriting prowess, and your live performance chops cemented my admiration, and your song catalog has been the soundtrack as I grew up, married my husband, Andrew, and became mom to our lovely girls, who are now sixteen and nineteen. Your music is, quite simply, a weft thread through a life made richer because of it.

But there are a lot of musicians whose music I love. What makes me especially grateful for yours is that it has brought great adventure into my life.

Between the "Six Months in a Leaky Boat" video and the beautiful voices of the Te Waka Huia Cultural Group Choir on your album *Together Alone*, a visit to New Zealand always held the top slot on my bucket list. So, in 2009, when the kids were eight and eleven, Andrew and I flew with them to Auckland and spent two weeks careening around the North Island in a camper van (including an hour in your hometown of Te Awamutu at the "History Never Repeats" exhibit in the town museum).

A few years after the NZ trip, Hilton Hotels ran an essay contest—"What act do you never miss when they come to town?" I dashed off 500 words and sent it, along with a picture of my coffee mug full of Finn-related ticket stubs, and when the 2014 Grammys rolled around, Andrew and I were there as Hilton's VIP all-expenses-paid winners. That experience was flat-out ridiculous in all the best ways, and we are so grateful that our Finn ticket stubs made it happen.

Other trips to catch you playing in LA at the Largo and the Troubadour with Andrew or with my girlfriends have added to my sense that I'd have many fewer frequent flyer miles if you weren't such a good songwriter.

I can't promise that sending these letters will yield any sort of response, especially if, like me, you feel compelled to write to dead people or celebrities. Rihanna may be your spirit animal, but that woman is BUSY.

I received a gracious email from Sheffield, and when my sister-in-law Suzanne saw him speak at a book festival in Texas, he inscribed one of his books with "Thank you Nancyyyy You are the Greatest." I've requested it be tucked into my coffin after I pass away listening to a Crowded House album during a post—ice cream nap at age ninety-three.

You should still write to these people. Say it with me: this project is about reminding yourself how you are held up, inspired, and supported each day as much as it is about thanking the people who perform that magic for you. Your recipients don't have to read these gratitude letters for them to work on you.

That said, I believe it is worth sending these letters to your role models when you can. You can probably find a mailing address if you want to send them, care of an agency or team or gallery. The immediacy of interactions on Twitter or Facebook between creators and fans is thrilling, it is true—that original MTV VJ Martha Quinn and I have become friendly thanks to Twitter remains one of the things I hope to someday time-travel back and tell my fifteen-year-old self.

But that is precisely why a carefully considered physical gratitude letter may stand out to this category of your recipients. It isn't done much these days. And if you do hear back, it will mean something special to you, too.

In the Neighborhood

By now you should be knee-deep in it, starting to see and recognize the people in your life who have worked to make it better. If you have been writing these gratitude letters, you are also well familiar with the tingle of anticipatory joy that happens when you drop the letter into the mailbox or press it into the recipient's hands, knowing that someone you value, admire, and appreciate is about to find out the exact reasons why that is the case. It almost feels like a secret superpower.

Why not keep your cape on a little longer?

Does your postal carrier hold your mail when you go out of town, even if you don't fill out the form right? Does the guy who runs your local market spot you a couple dollars when you forget your wallet? Where would you be without the babysitter who is willing to play Polly Pocket or LEGO with your three-year-old for hours at a time, when you are ready to tap out from boredom after twelve minutes?

In the latter category I had to write a gratitude letter to Helle, the wonderful young woman who babysat our children when they were small. She is a gifted artist who made entire detailed paper-doll casts of whatever television shows or stories the girls were obsessed with at the time (including *Pride and Prejudice*, obviously), offered to assemble our Ikea furniture for us when the girls napped, and was, some days, the only adult I spoke with besides Andrew.

> By sharing your affection, creativity, and amazing patience with our daughters, I know you helped make them the bright, kind, and affectionate young women they are. And I will always be grateful to you for that.
>
> Remember Lucy's famous line at age three? "I don't care if she is a grown-up. Helle's my best friend."
>
> Now that you're a mom yourself, I hope you can fully appreciate the difference it makes for a working mom to have that kind of support and trust with her babysitter. I hope you recognize and applaud yourself for making that possible not just for me, but for all the moms whose children you watched over the years.

Hairdressers, dry cleaners, waitresses, auto mechanics: your deliberate thanks to the helpers around you, the ones who really grease the wheels of your day-to-day life without expecting anything extra in return, carries so much power. And all it takes is a bit of your time and a blank piece of paper to kick it into gear.

INSPIRATION FROM INFLUENCERS

A

My Hero—Foo Fighters

Angels—Chance the Rapper
  feat. Saba

When You Believe—Whitney
  Houston and Mariah Carey

Sweet Inspiration—Diana Ross &
  The Supremes and
  The Temptations

Let the Day Begin—The Call

Just Got Paid—Johnny Kemp

Big Boss Lady—John Lee Hooker

B

Take This Job and Shove It—
  Johnny Paycheck

Heroes—David Bowie

Positive Role Model—Pet Shop Boys

Leader of the Band—Dan Fogelberg

You're the Inspiration—Chicago

My Heroes Have Always Been
  Cowboys—Willie Nelson

Tip That Waitress—Loudon
  Wainwright III

Motivate—Matisyahu

CHAPTER 6

PRAISE FOR PLACES AND PASTIMES

Give thanks for a little, and you will find a lot.
—HAUSA PROVERB FROM WEST AFRICA

As I neared the end of my letter-writing project, my ability to identify the people in my life who were worthy of a gratitude letter had gotten sharper—so much so that I realized they weren't all people. If the criterion for a letter was to recognize entities that had shaped and formed me, then there were places I have lived, and things I have loved, that were equally deserving of recognition. And even if none of the recipients in this section of my letters had an actual street address, what with being inanimate and all, I knew by then that savoring the reasons each of those entities meant so much to me would be its own reward.

I started with places I had lived. Not all of them; I had a short stint in Quebec City that was memorable for a scary Peeping Tom encounter, a seagull that struggled to make off with a tourist's ice cream cone only to drop it on my head, and an unhinged woman who flashed a butcher's knife at me on a deserted street. No letter for you, Quebec City! Though Château Frontenac sure is pretty.

I wrote letters to the places where I had stayed long enough to be imprinted, or where I had learned lessons from which I still benefit, or where I go even now for peace and perspective. Here are a few of those types of places you might consider.

Hometowns

I have lived away from Rochester, New York, for twice as long as I ever lived there. But it was the first place to which I wrote a gratitude letter, which is ironic because growing up on the shores of Lake Ontario, trapped in the embrace of "lake-effect snow" six months of the year, I spent most of my time yearning to be anywhere else.

It was a clear-cut case of not knowing how good I had it until I could look at Rochester from a distance. For a kid who wished her life looked like an MTV music video, any MTV music video, it was not the most exciting city. It only offered safe streets, top-notch public schools, easy access to parks and trails, and the world's greatest grocery store, Wegmans. You know, nothing that matters when you are a fifteen-year-old dummy.

Once I moved away, it finally began to dawn on me not just how much Rochester offered, but how deeply the city's personality was woven into my DNA. As a "Kodakid"—i.e., someone whose parent was an employee of Eastman Kodak, the company that cast its yellow-and-red shadow over our whole city—the company's prolonged decline felt oddly personal to me. Rochester's continued survival, despite Kodak's bankruptcy and the loss of more than a hundred thousand jobs in the city in the waning years of the twentieth century, feels the same way. Frankly, it's why I always look bitter in Polaroid pictures.

When I wrote my letter to my hometown, I said:

Even if I've now lived in Oakland longer than I ever did in Roch, you are and always will be what I picture when I think of "home."

For a long time, I've said of you, "It was a wonderful place to grow up. And a wonderful place to be from." As in, for me, I had to move away to fully appreciate your charms. My siblings and I grew up on a modest street where everyone tended their yard, no one locked their doors, and the kids roamed outside like a pack of feral, if harmless, animals monitored by everyone else's parents. We attended public schools that we could walk to, we biked to our after-school jobs, we went on dates to "the city"—i.e., Rochester—a full five minutes' drive from the suburbs of Brighton.

I cannot tell you how grateful I am to have had that predictable, secure, normal childhood. I think part of the reason I'm temperamentally down to earth is because I grew up in such a humble, no-drama place. There was no point in being conceited about Rochester, nor being apologetic either. It wasn't glamorous, but it was sturdy, and that was more than enough.

I was gone by the time Kodak entered the final death spiral, but from a distance I want to say that I admire Rochester's tenaciousness and determination not to become a victim of economic tides. Whenever I go back, there are new businesses being opened and old ones hanging on. It's not meteor-ride-velocity, but, again, it's enough to keep moving forward.

I think I knew by age fourteen that it wouldn't be the place I lived forever, but especially in the past year I've been grateful for the increased number and length of visits there to stay with Mom. It will feel so, so strange when I don't have her home to visit anymore. But I don't think Mom's eventual absence will keep me from feeling that sense of "aaaaaaaahhhhh, home" that washes over me every time I step off the plane into the Rochester airport. It's soaked too deeply into my pores.

So, Rochester, thanks for everything you gave me growing up on your safe, quiet streets. I wouldn't change a thing.

Your hometown may be another example of a force in your life that helped you clarify what you did not want. It's funny: where I looked at Rochester and wanted a faster pace as a grown-up, my sister, Sally, had the opposite reaction. She ended up moving to rural Maine and spent a happy decade there in a small town surrounded by tall green pine trees, the scent of woodstove smoke in the air. Meanwhile, my brother, Larry, bought a home less than two miles from the house in which we grew up, and his children attended the same schools that we did. Same inputs, different conclusions. How does the place you are from inform the choices you make today?

"Hometown" is as "hometown" does. If you moved a lot as a kid, maybe there's a town that felt more like home than the others, or maybe each stop on your geographic path lent something to the person you are now and deserves its own meditation of gratitude.

Depending on where you grew up, you could write a whole letter just dedicated to the cuisine of your hometown. Since the most famous culinary masterpiece of my hometown is called "The Garbage Plate"—baked beans, topped by macaroni salad, topped by meat, topped by heartburn and regret—I gave that one a pass. But I am proud to come from a city where Frederick Douglass and Susan B. Anthony chose to live, that hosts a wonderful Lilac Festival every spring, and that regards temperatures higher than 45 degrees as "shorts weather."

Here's another way to think about it: if you were a realtor trying to sell someone on the attributes of the place(s) you grew up, what are the first things you would mention? And how have those properties shaped who you are now?

The Places That Changed You

Perhaps it was a short vacation. Maybe it was a temporary relocation. It could have been one of those moments when you went someplace for the first time only to realize that you were finally home. What are the physical places through which you have passed in your life that left a lasting impression?

It was easy for me to know the first letter to write in this category: Camp Gorham. Since I was a toddler, my family has spent the last week in August in the Adirondack Mountains at a weeklong family camp run by the Rochester YMCA. Think *Dirty Dancing* without Patrick Swayze, white linen tablecloths, or the backroom abortion story line. We head there along with about thirty-five other families, many of whom have also been attending since before man first landed on the moon. As a teen, I worked as a counselor for the kids' camping program that runs all summer, and Maddy eventually followed in my footsteps. Meanwhile, my father became the self-appointed camp historian. Family Camp is rustic, retro, and, quite simply, my favorite place in the world to be. I wrote:

Family Camp, it's going to be hard to express how central you have been to my life—as a daughter, a sister, an aunt, a wife, and a mom. Mom and Dad started taking the Davis Five there in 1968, when I was two, and I don't remember a thing about that trip. But from the moment my folks decided to overlook the legendary Flying Squirrel Incident and take us back for a second year, Gorham became our family's special sauce.

I truly believe this. Once a year, we all do our damndest to get back there—as do most of our kids. It is, of course, a place of great physical beauty and a week in which we get to push ourselves physically, up mountains and in lakes and atop horses. But more than that, it's a place where we all still play together, even as grown-ups. The camaraderie and affection that gets reinforced with every afternoon spent on the porch of Laurel Cabin, every square dance, every late-night game of pool at one of the nearby taverns is, I think, a giant part of why the Davis family genuinely likes one another.

Most of my friends don't have a place like this, where the siblings can spend time together but also apart, where the cousins who don't see each other much bond in a tight time frame, where traditions are hokey (and frequently pokey) but remind us of how long we've been and will be connected to one another. We may scatter to the four winds during the year, but it's vastly reassuring to know that during the last week of August, most of my nearest and dearest will be driving down the Big Moose Road at 12:49 p.m., pushing the 1 p.m. arrival time as close as they dare.

The time I knew Andrew was really for me was when I brought him to camp and he didn't like it much—and even THAT didn't make me love him any less. The fact that he put his own preferences aside and made this a family vacation for our kids over the years says everything about who I married. I have never been so turned on as the year he participated in (and thankfully survived) the mercenary Men's Kayak Race, without my even suggesting it.

Both Maddy and Lu got hefty doses of that wonderful Family Camp gift of childhood freedom—those precious weeks when they were little when they could roam your 1,500 splendid acres more freely than we could let them in Oakland, accompanied only by their cousins or even on their own. We were confident (and rightfully so) that they would be fine, or someone would help them if they needed it. I witnessed this in my nieces and nephews too—those gulps of liberty at a young age that accelerated their self-sufficiency in a profound way.

Lulu may be more of her father's daughter when it comes to what Andrew refers to as "the camp gene," but Maddy got the bug, bad. As of this summer she'll have worked there as a counselor three years in a row—longer than I ever did. I love to see her light up in excitement about going there, and I know that my dad was so proud of her work there. I will always remember taking him up to deliver his annual Camp History lecture to the staff in June last year, at the midpoint between his diagnosis and his death. That day was a gift to all of us.

So, Family Camp, see you the last week in August. Until the day I die.

Is there a special vacation spot you go to year after year, or a place that seemed to rewire you after only one visit? If someone handed you a free plane, train, or bus ticket with the stipulation that you had to go somewhere that you have visited already, where would you return, and why? You might even write a gratitude letter to a place you still dream of seeing for the first time, Machu Picchu or the Great Barrier Reef or Yellowstone Park. I find the act of looking forward to a vacation almost as satisfying as actually taking one, and it is certainly cheaper.

In this category you might also write to the schools and programs where you studied or trained. One of my letters was to the graduate school I attended outside of Phoenix, called Thunderbird. (Go ahead, make jokes about cheap wine and old cars here;

all Tbird grads are accustomed to taking a pause at this point in the conversation.) Housed on an old World War II pilot-training facility that had been laid out in the shape of the mythical bird, Thunderbird's proper name was the American Graduate School of International Management. The graduate school opened after World War II ended, and its mission was to educate business-people to be global citizens. Thunderbird attracted a niche student: ambitious, but really into foreign-language study, international relations, and imported beer available from the on-campus pub. In other words, me.

I applied to Thunderbird while I was living in Munich, and I moved to Phoenix having never seen the campus before and knowing not a soul. When I left eighteen months later, I had a fiancé, a job in international business, and a whole new pack of like-minded Tbird friends who prioritized new passport stamps and the ability to say "Cheers!" in the local language over every other achievement. I wrote:

When I arrived in August 1990, I drove straight to Greentree Apartments across the street from school, the place I'd rented sight unseen, and didn't cross 59th Street onto campus until I had to. I was so nervous that it wouldn't live up to the hype.

My fears couldn't have been more misplaced. Thunderbird is, simply put, where I found my tribe, or at least the tribe I needed at that point in my life. First, of course, was Andrew. If all you'd ever brought into my life was my globally minded, travel-loving husband, I would owe you a great debt of thanks. My second semester of school there, I basically majored in falling in love with that guy, and it was one of the happiest periods of my whole life.

But Thunderbird is also where I met Pam, Ledette, Miles, Carolyn, Ann, Sarah, Hugh, JJ, Z-man, and a whole host of other friends who remain in my life and with whom I will always share bonds made over language labs, International Political Economy classes, and dry heat. I credit the school for taking my nascent interest in being a global citizen and firing it into a life philosophy. In its heyday, Thunderbird made us both proud to be American and proud to be part of a larger universe of people who truly believed that William Schurz quote: "Borders frequented by trade seldom need soldiers."

We developed a mindset of outreach, understanding, and mutual enrichment that is still—or maybe even more— needed now. As Tbirds, we also developed a healthy sense of balance: class in the morning, study your butt off in the afternoon, do a run in the evening after the temperature drops, and stop by the pub to "hydrate" on the way home.

The last time we visited campus was for the big rededication of the funky air control tower and the new pub about five years ago—sadly, the hallowed ground of the old pub where Andrew and I first met is no more. Since then, of course, Thunderbird has been absorbed into the business school of Arizona State University, a fact I try not to find heartbreaking.

But that in no way lessens the gratitude I feel for the very real ways in which Thunderbird expanded my horizons.

If you attended a school that put you on a particular career path or was the place you met close friends or pushed you to understand just how hard you are capable of working, a gratitude letter might be a useful way to reflect on how that impacts your life today.

The final "place" letter I wrote was to Oakland, the city where I live now. I love this burg with all my heart and despite all its imperfections, and it has rubbed off on me in so many wonderful ways during my two decades here.

This is a thank-you note to the city where I have lived for nearly twenty years. It's the longest I have lived anywhere. To think that when Andrew and I moved here in 1997, I whispered to my mom as I hugged her goodbye, "Don't worry. It's only for three years."

Oakland, you're the freshest. If I am hip at all at age fifty, it's because as a city you make it so easy and desirable to remain tuned in, engaged, vibrant. I'm amazed at the transformation that's taken place in the last ten years, as Oakland chips away at San Francisco's appeal with each new cool restaurant, club, First Friday festival, concert. We almost never go across the Bay Bridge into San Francisco for entertainment; why would you need to? Between concerts at the Fox Theater, hikes in Redwood Park, lazy lunches at Lost & Found and dinner at Duende, movies on Piedmont Avenue—there's nothing San Francisco offers that Oakland doesn't except worse traffic and more expensive parking.

I think it's Oakland's can't-quite-make-it streak that makes me love you as I do. God bless you for trying, all the time. A lesser city would know to give up in the face of some of our odds (and I do mean "odd"). Oakland's just like, "OK, that didn't work! Now what?!" I love our enthusiasm, our diversity, our well-meaning intentions that clash with our funding limits. I love our warm winters and our cool summers. I love our Warriors, even if they're leaving us to move to San Francisco, and I love our A's, even if I manage one game a year in a good year. (I never think about the Raiders, but it's not personal. Sorry, and enjoy Las Vegas.)

I love our openness and our edginess and our public schools where our girls have been exposed to every kind of diversity: economic, racial, gender identity, sexual orientation. I love that we raise activists who will fight for things to be better. I don't love living on top of the Hayward fault, but I appreciate that in twenty years the worst quake I've suffered is a 5.5, and I don't even get out of bed for something less than a 4.3.

Andrew and I talk about where we'll go after the nest is empty: Burlington, Vermont? Petaluma? San Francisco? Berkeley? But if I'm honest, I'd stay right here in the 5-1-0, being the hippest old lady around and soaking up the sun and the funky vibes. Thanks, Oakland, for being home to me and my family.

Other "place" letters you might write? How about to your first apartment, the one that taught you the joys and tribulations of living away from your parents for the first time, not to mention the fun of negotiating kitchen chores with your roommate(s)? What about the nearby park where you take your morning run and get your head on straight every day? You could even write to a place you will never go again because you had such a lousy time, and now you know to avoid those kinds of tourist traps during the high season. Hey, Walley World isn't for everyone.

Passions and Pursuits

We have now arrived at the Oprah-inspired "You get a letter! You get a letter! You get a letter!" portion of the gratitude-letter project, where we are literally writing letters to concepts and ideas. I'm not just telling you this to waste paper, I swear.

You are a unique person, with so many interesting facets to your life. What are the other things that make you YOU? Or to rephrase the questions from the beginning of the book:

What has shaped me?
What has helped me?
What has inspired me?

The hobbies we engage in, the interests that give us a sense of purpose, the passions we pursue all contribute to the person we are. Take a moment to consider the richness that those things bring to your life, and you will likely find much to be grateful for.

Anyone who knows me knows that I love live music and concerts. I try to go to one every month, and I cast the net wide with Americana acts, indie rockers, eighties bands going out on yet another reunion tour, and the occasional rap show, if only to make the security guards gasp in surprise at my posse of aging mom rap fans. (Hey, before we were middle-aged parents, we were the kids at the Run DMC, Public Enemy, and Beastie Boys shows. I still bust mad moves; I just have to tuck my reading glasses away first.)

Naturally, when I made my list of letters, I included the names of various bands to whom I would write. It quickly became clear that this was either going to be a nine-year letter-writing project or I would need to consolidate. Hence, my letter to the live music industry.

To All the Bands I've Loved Before:
I intended to write a letter to Lord Huron, then Liz Phair, then Echo and the Bunnymen, then Brandi Carlile, then Frank Turner, and and and . . . and then I realized I would be saying the same thing in all of them. Thank you, talented musicians, for the richness and community and energy you've brought into my life.

Science shows that music impacts the human brain in myriad positive ways; I think I was born with the wiring a little more sensitive than most. To put it another way, I just care about music. It matters to me. I listen to it a lot, I think about it even more, and about ten years ago I realized that going out to hear live music was one of the few ways I could reconnect with my youth in a meaningful way. Going to a show doesn't make me feel twenty-one, but it helps me remember what I was like at that age. And in a lot of ways, that's part of why I'm grateful to be fifty. I wouldn't want to be in my twenties again. I'm more confident, experienced, and have deeper relationships now than I did three decades ago. But if I weren't occasionally reminded of that twenty-year-old girl, I might take all the fifty-ish-ness of myself for granted.

I'm constantly inspired by your creativity in songwriting, your mastery as musicians, and your energy in touring and performing. I come away from almost every concert feeling like I've spent a couple minutes or hours in the presence of God-given creative talents, situations in which the Divine and the everyday collide. Concerts are a spiritual practice for me in this sense, and I know I'd be a less complete person without them.

I appreciate the way your songs buoy a low mood, amplify a good one, and express feelings that are beyond words. The right song at the right time is better than pharmaceuticals.

For all these reasons and more, I am grateful to you, the musicians who have enriched my fifty years. Thank you from the bottom of my dancing shoes.

What is it for you? Fly-fishing, or scrapbooking, or re-creating recipes you saw on television cooking shows? What is the thing that causes you to wake up early and think, "Today's the day!"

After reading an early version of this book, my friend Ann called to tell me she realized she needed more "Today's the day!" in her life, and it prompted her to get herself back into voice lessons.

Ann, who has a background in musical theater, founded

Listen to Your Mother, a live storytelling series produced in more than fifty cities that sought to "give motherhood a microphone." When the curtain closed on her involvement with the show after seven years, she felt a still, small urge to sing again—in effect, to give herself a microphone.

"I felt so nervous about taking singing seriously," she told me, having been away from it for more than twenty years as she reoriented her career and raised two sons. "After giving myself 100 reasons why I do not need voice coaching, I reconsidered it anyway—for accountability, to get me singing, and because frankly even though I love my life, I need more energy and joy. If I schedule a lesson, I will prepare for that lesson." *Today's the day I get to sing!* And then, maybe afterward, write a letter?

It doesn't have to be a big hoopla for something to merit your gratitude and attention, and maybe one of your letters. On Sunday mornings, when Andrew arrives home from the lone bagel bakery in Northern California that understands bagels are not simply white bread rolls with holes poked in the middle, I have to admit to getting that flutter of delight. Today's the day for a toasted sesame bagel with schmear!

Imagine how flat your life would be without your specific interests and passions. Then, pick up a pen and celebrate that you don't have to live that way.

PRAISE FOR PLACES
AND PASTIMES

In My City—Mistah F.A.B.
  Daveed Diggs, and Rafael Casal
WTF (Where They From)—Missy
  Elliott feat. Pharrell Williams
My Hometown—Bruce Springsteen
Rivers—Frank Turner
Life in a Northern Town—
  The Dream Academy
Sweet Home Alabama—
  Lynyrd Skynyrd
Viva Las Vegas—Elvis Presley
Tennessee—Arrested Development

Route 66—Nat King Cole
Vacation—The Go-Gos
Paint It Black—Rolling Stones
  cover by Echo & The Bunnymen
I Made the Prison Band—
  Merle Haggard
Whatever Happened to Pong?—
  Frank Black
Fruit Nut—XTC
Mein Hobby sind die Girls—
  Die Roten Rosen

CHAPTER 7

NOW, IT'S YOUR TURN

When I started counting my blessings,
my whole life turned around.

—WILLIE NELSON

By now you have been writing letters for weeks, months, perhaps even years. But only now are you getting to the most important letter of this project: the one you write to yourself. It's the Big Kahuna of letters, the capstone, The End. And there is a good reason you write to yourself last.

As with so many aspects of this project, I did not see the significance of this in advance. But as the letters added up over time, as I documented the mosaic of support I had created in my fifty years, I took the bold step of adding my own name on the last line of my list. And I am requesting that you do the same because you, too, deserve a thank-you.

First, you helped sustain the US Postal Service for a little while longer with all those stamp purchases. As someone who genuinely looks forward to seeing the new Ikea catalog land in my mailbox every September, I'm grateful to you for that. I'm thinking of springing for a SJÖPENNA for the living room this year.

Second, look at all those words you put on paper! You undertook a significant writing project with these letters, and not even for a grade. The first book I ever wrote, which remains in a drawer for good reason, was a historical-fiction epic requiring years of research and at least six drafts. In its final, lumbering form, it clocked in at some 127,000 words. When I had finally finished it, we invited our friends Carolyn and Keao for dinner, and Keao offered a toast I still remember with delight. He raised his glass and said, "Here's to you! You typed 421 pages!"

Here's to you! You produced [Insert Your Number Here] thank-you notes! You deserve some recognition from yourself for that.

But, of course, the main reason you write a letter to yourself is for the magic of what is captured in the letters you wrote.

Your recipients are kind, amazing, interesting people who have generously given of themselves to help you over the years. Or they are the opposite, and you have turned that into useful life instruction nonetheless. You have written to people, places, and pastimes that may not have much in common with each other but that together create a one-of-a-kind safety net that has brought you to where you are today.

Now, who is the artist behind the masterpiece that is your unique support network?

YOU, Common Denominator! You are awesome. Look at what you have pulled off.

Remember that definition of gratitude from Dr. Emmons

at the beginning of the book? It includes recognition that the source of goodness in your life lies "*at least partially* outside the self." Italics mine, baby. He is saying that at least part of the source of goodness in your life is *inside* the self. *José! It's finally all about you!*

Before you write this final letter, take some time to reread all that you have written. Go through your letters and take a big, heady inhale, not just of who your people, places, and pastimes are, but the knowledge that you took the time to let them know what they mean to you.

In an era characterized by brokenness and isolation, you built yourself a no-emissions, solar-powered gratitude factory to put healing, positive energy into a world badly in need of more of it. You may even have inspired some of your recipients to write their own letters. That upward spiral of gratitude and happiness? You caused that.

Something else may have happened as you considered and wrote your letters: you may have realized that it was time to clean house, relationship-wise. This letter-writing practice has a sneaky way of making you better, stronger, and faster at figuring out what active support and healthy relationships look like for you, and less patient with putting up with those that fall short. That is OK. That is great. That is growth.

And then you can start writing this final letter. What did you learn from your letters, about yourself and about your relationships? Where did you perhaps find clarity and closure? Have you experienced a shift in your ability to recognize that, even in the worst of circumstances and times, there are good things for which you can be grateful?

I wrote the letter to myself on the morning of my fifty-first birthday, more than a year after I had sat down to write Mom and Dad my very first two thank-you letters. Here's what I said:

Dear Nancy:
And thus endeth the mid-century year of deliberate gratitude.

This project has been so much more than I expected it to be—a chance to reflect, a tool for optimism, a means of measuring accomplishment. To my friends I've said that age fifty was a roller coaster of good and bad, and it's true. So much to be grateful for, from the birthday celebrations to Maddy's high school graduation and her happiness at college, to Lucy's continuing to thrive, to the hiking trip Andrew and I took to celebrate our twenty-fifth anniversary.

And so much to mourn: losing Dad, a process bigger and longer than a year could ever contain.

I could start all over again tomorrow and write thank-you notes to the same people, and more, and still never get to the bottom of the well of gratitude. If nothing else, I hope that what I've done here is create a habit of noticing and being thankful that I'll carry into the next half of my life.

Happy fifty-first, Nancy. You have so much to celebrate.

Whether this letter is your fiftieth or your twentieth or your hundredth, promise me you will set aside a time to write a thank-you letter to yourself. And once it is done, remember to compile all your letters together, so you can fan them toward your face like a homemade wind machine.

Because you rock for putting all that juicy transformative gratitude into the world, and it is only fitting you blow your hair backward like you're the star of your very own music video.

NOW, IT'S YOUR TURN

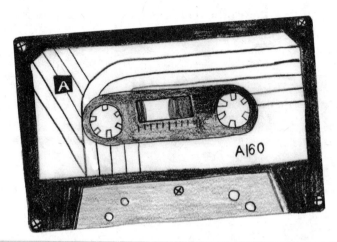

 A

Over the Rainbow/What a
Wonderful World—
Israel 'IZ' Kamakawio'ole
Letter to Me—Brad Paisley
Me, Myself, I—
Joan Armatrading
Soy Yo—Bomba Estéreo
The Best—Tina Turner
Glorious You—Frank Turner
Express Yourself—Madonna

 B

Story of My Life—Social Distortion
Once in a Lifetime—Talking Heads
Complicated—Poi Dog Pondering
All My Mistakes—
The Avett Brothers
True Colors—Cyndi Lauper
Sheila Take a Bow—The Smiths
Happiness—Blue Nile
Don't Dream It's Over—
Crowded House

CHAPTER 8

DEAR READER

Dear Reader:

We likely do not know one another personally, so it may feel strange to receive a thank-you letter from me. But I have been writing a book about how expressing gratitude to the important people and things in your life can cultivate happiness, and as I reach the end of said book it is clear to me that you, Dear Reader, deserve a thank-you from me.

First, I am appreciative that you have taken the time to read my writing. There are a million demands on your time, and I am not even counting kitten and puppy videos. I do not take for granted that you were kind enough to spend some of it reading the work I have written. I am rather late to the game to become a debut author, but it gave me a chance to teach a valuable lesson to Maddy and Lucy about sticking with a dream and putting in the hard work until you reach it, no matter how long it takes.

Second, in writing this book, I got the chance to retrace the path of my own thank-you-letter writing project. Now I know I stopped it too soon. The exercise of thinking through all the various people and things that a diverse group of readers might want to include on their own list of gratitude letters made me realize there were so many additional names that should have been on mine, and that fifty was a short-sighted goal. I'm mortified to admit this but . . . I never actually wrote to Mrs. Green of my AP English class, or Brenda, my exemplary dot-com boss. In the time that has passed since I finished my Thank-You Project, I started taking a hip-hop class in Oakland that makes me wake up every Saturday and think, "Today's the day!"

Thanks to you, Dear Reader, I have a spiral notebook sitting next to me here at my desk with a whole list of names of additional people and things to write to, including Mrs. Green, Brenda, and Saturday hip-hop class. Beauty Bagels on Telegraph Avenue in Oakland: thank-you letter coming in hot. I'm going to call this *The Thank-You Letters: Volume 2.* Or *The Return of the Thank-You Letters.* (I feel like *Son of Thank-You Letters* is overly aggressive.)

Finally, the same week that I found a publisher for this book, my beloved eighty-four-year-old mom was diagnosed with cancer. As of this writing, she is managing fine, with lots of support from Larry and Sally and their families, and there are treatment options that promise to extend both the quality of her life and its duration. I fly out to see her in Rochester next week to try to be helpful.

But I am struck by the symmetry of how I wrote my original gratitude letters during the year I lost my dad, and how I wrote a how-to book about those gratitude letters as my mom received a difficult diagnosis. Once again, the

gratitude letters have steadied me. Once again, medita-
tions on gratitude have helped me crowd out thoughts of
fear and sadness, at least for the time it took to put my
thoughts on paper during each pre-dawn writing session.

And although Mom's cognitive decline marches on, the
day she said to me on the phone, clear as can be, "What's
this I hear about you writing a book?" That? That was a
great day. Without you, it wouldn't have been possible.

As I explained to Maria's husband, Ted, another name
on my *Volume 2* list, about the incongruity of having such
wonderful and terrible news in the same season, "I'd rather
have it be Best of Times/Worst of Times than Worst of
Times/Worst of Times." These gratitude letters—both as
you write them and as you reread and savor what you
have written in the weeks, months, and years to come—
are a way to manufacture your own Best of Times on an
as-needed basis. I have now proven that theory twice.

So, thank you from the bottom of my heart, Dear
Reader, for all the ways in which you have enriched my life.
I hope that this letter finds you well. Let's grab a coffee
and catch up soon, OK?

Thanks again for everything,

Nan

ACKNOWLEDGMENTS

Sure, write some acknowledgments for a book about the importance of expressing appreciation. No pressure there.

Thanks to Ann Imig and Lara Starr for the one-two punch of "you know, this letter-writing thing you did could be a book." I'm grateful to Ann, Maria Hjelm, KJ Dell'Antonia, Lisa Page Rosenberg, Glynis Mason, Laurie White, Michelle Cruz Gonzales, and Michelle Villegas Threadgould for editorial input on tight turnarounds along the way.

I am so grateful for the able guidance of Jennifer Kasius and the Running Press team, and to Laurie Abkemeier for sticking with me to find the right story for the right publishing home. I feel lucky to have such a crack team working with me. Carole Bidnick and Amy Williams cheered me on along the way, literary class and kindness personified.

Dr. Christine Carter of the Greater Good Science Center at UC Berkeley and Dr. Kristin Layous at California State University East Bay were generous with their research, insights, and encouragement about the science of gratitude and happiness along the way, for which I am—you guessed it—grateful and happy. Melisa Wells and Dr. Shannon Connery kindly shared stories and reactions from their own gratitude projects, and Kathy Valentine took time from her busy performing schedule to describe the impact of handing out thank-you letters at her fiftieth birthday party. Catch her playing with the Blue Bonnets next time you're in Austin, folks.

Little did I understand when I moved to the Bay Area in 1997 that I was dropping into the most supportive, inspiring literary community in the world, where diverse stories are sought, cultivated, and amplified. Over the years my writing has been honed and championed by the overlapping writing communities of Lit Camp, Litquake, the San Francisco Writer's Grotto, *Listen to Your Mother*, Book Passage's Travel Writing Conference, Literary Death Match, The Writing Salon, Moxie Road Productions, and Adair Lara's cozy living room. In each, I've learned from generous, skilled instructors and fellow writers about this craft to which we are devoted. Brooke Warner has been an invaluable source of writing wisdom throughout, across topics and projects. Over the years, the Erma Bombeck Writing Workshop, Mom2.0, and BlogHer conferences have always left me feeling smarter and inspired to work even harder.

I'm grateful to all the editors with whom I've worked at the *San Francisco Chronicle, Washington Post,* and the other editorial outlets that have published my work. It's a privilege to receive your feedback and guidance.

Thank you, Kathleen Caldwell and A Great Good Place for Books in Oakland, for providing my indie bookstore version of *Cheers.* Good writers must first be good readers, and Kathleen makes it easy by having a recommendation ready whenever I walk through the door. GGP (and indie bookstores in general) create an invaluable space for writers and readers to connect, both on the page and in person.

This book would never have left my hard drive were it not for the constant and comprehensive support given me by Maria Hjelm and Jill McCleary, the Hella Housewives, and the Tiny Texters. You gals are simply the most; please see your individual thank-you letters for supporting arguments. Thea Sullivan, Muffy

Srinivasan, Bruce Feiler, and Mary Laura Philpott chimed in with the right advice at the right time, too.

It's hard to find words big enough to thank my sister, Sally Berry, and my brother, Larry Davis, and their families, who provided me the most meaningful gift I could ask for while I wrote this book: peace of mind that our mom was being cared for. They even had extra energy left over to read early drafts and give me feedback. First round at the Glenmore on the first night of Family Camp next year is on me, guys.

I'm grateful to my mom, Laura Davis, for gifting me the love of reading that led to a love of writing. Every Wednesday while we were in grade school, she went to the library to select a stack of books for Sally, Larry, and me to read over the next seven days. Mom, it finally paid off! My mother-in-law, Helen Kho, has been an enthusiastic cheerleader as well.

And finally, to Andrew, Maddy, and Lucy: thank you for your constant love and your support of this dream I've had for so many years. As they definitely do not say in Ireland, *Solange!*